HOW TO
F*CK A
WOMAN

HOW TO F*CK A WOMAN

*An Insider's Guide to Love and Relationships

Ali Adler

WEINSTEIN
BOOKS

Printed in the United States of America.

Editorial production by *Marra*thon Production Services.
www.marrathon.net
Book design by Ellen Rosenblatt
Set in 11.5 point Giovanni

Cataloging-in-Publication data for this book is available
from the Library of Congress.

ISBN: 978-1-60286-282-1 (print)
ISBN: 978-1-60286-283-8 (e-book)

Published by Weinstein Books
A member of the Perseus Books Group
www.weinsteinbooks.com

Weinstein Books are available at special discounts for bulk purchases
in the U.S. by corporations, institutions and other organizations.
For more information, please contact the Special Markets Department
at the Perseus Books Group, 2300 Chestnut Street, Suite 200,
Philadelphia, PA 19103, call (800) 810–4145, ext. 5000,
or e-mail special.markets@perseusbooks.com.

First edition

10 9 8 7 6 5 4 3 2 1

To my kids. If someday you read this,
even if you're very embarrassed
I was the one to say it, know that it had to be said.
And to Elizabeth, my best and final.

Contents

Contents

HOW TO
F*CK A
WOMAN

"Good—just like that, but with me."

Introduction

Women aren't really from Venus. They make up more than half the Earth's population. You share your bed with some of them. Yet, even after years of friendship or working together or dating or fucking or love or marriage, most men still don't seem to understand some of the more basic things about women. And I don't blame you for not knowing this stuff, even if other women might. I mean, you can't guess what you never knew. And who are you supposed to ask? Certainly not women, because they'll judge you for your lack of knowledge.

You wonder why she's always worried about things that aren't happening. You wonder why she's always cold when you're always hot. You wonder why she gets so upset over what seem to be little things. You don't understand why she never stops planning in advance or sniffing out strange odors that you never even smell. You don't understand why she needs to be in constant communication, when you just want a little goddamn silence.

The thing is, she wonders all these same things in the reverse about you. Plus the bonus enigma of why, after all these years, you don't seem to know how to touch her clitoris with the sensitivity it desperately begs for. So many of these mysteries are pretty simple once they're explained, and I've covered them in this book. The fantastic thing is, once you learn the answers to these questions and many more, you can begin reaping the benefits of your knowledge by living a much more peaceful life. One that includes way more fucking.

So. What are my qualifications? Well, I do know the parts because I've owned the equipment all my life. I mean, if you were born with a Rubik's Cube in your underpants, you'd sure as hell figure out how to master it over time. I'm not only referring to the parts here; I've also owned the temperament. It comes free with the vagina. Like the set of steak knives you get as a bonus if you "act now." Plus, I'm gay. So, just like you, I'm attracted to women. Yes, I'm also occasionally confounded by my own gender, but I am one, too, so I do have quite a bit of insider information.

⌒

The idea for this book came to me while I was a writer for a half-hour TV show. Often, these comedy rooms (the "writers' room") are a bastion of boys wearing hoodies in various states of elbow-holed disrepair. Testosterone, fear, competitive eating games, and flatulence fill the air. These types of rooms are all basically the same. An old conference table coated with SunChip- (née potato chip-) greasy fingerprints and ghosts of old jokes ("Frasier, your girlfriend is as young as this Beaujolais!"). The room has been repainted so many times, it's exponentially smaller because of it. Lots of guys sitting around in Dockers and pocket T-shirts, wholly unaware of any changes in fashion in the past decade, stuck in a time-bubble from before Banana Republic used gay-boys to do their ads.

I'm usually the only female writer (maybe one of a few) in a room filled with a dozen people. And I have a very privileged window into a world that most women don't get to absorb. I sit with them, and we all share the most intimate details of our lives. Invariably these rooms devolve into discussions of when was the last time you had sex, who you did it with, whose wife/girlfriend allows them rear privilege, and how much would you have to be paid to eat out the bunghole of the pot-bellied location scout. ("Did Gary bathe recently?" "How long would I have to eat it for?" "Does eating Gary's asshole make me gay, or just a whore?" "Do I have to get him off with my hand, or would he do it himself?" "Tax-wise, do I have to declare this as income, or would it come in bricks of cash in a shoebox?") Conversations that don't usually come up at work.

At some point in this decadent unproductive soup, the boys ask me to share every single sexual experience I've ever had. ("Because of two pussies!") One show I worked on made this a regular thing. They asked me to regale them every Friday. Like a library story-time for pervy dudes who missed out on sex in their teens because they were studying for their SATs. They called it "Lesbian Fridays," and they pined for it with the same kind of longing they had for dim-sum dumplings. Which, not so coincidentally, were also delivered on Fridays.

One of them always played moderator for this weekly occurrence of the discussion of my sexual escapades. He was like a no-sock-wearing, bespectacled, Jewish hipster Charlie Rose. One day, right before Christmas break, another one of the guys chimed in and offered a morsel about his own sexual prowess regarding his brand new bride: "Last night, I fucked her hard. Played with her clit—" And then I watched as he pantomimed his accompanying action. It looked like he was rapidly flipping on and off a very loose light switch. Like the signal to come back from intermission at an amateur playhouse.

I was shocked. As a woman who has sex with women, and as a woman who receives sexual pleasure, no part of me identified with the extreme finger calisthenics that he was demonstrating. I didn't want to shame him, but this had to stop. I had to put an end to this and probably other horrific things that, I could only assume, were being perpetrated in the bedrooms of men such as this.

I brushed powdered sugar Donette crumbs from my mouth. Took a sip of Coke, swishing the fizzing brown liquid all over my teeth. I stood up, resolved to set them straighter than they already were. They wondered what was happening as I closed the door of the room. Some asshole balked: the one who always shoved a *New York Times* in his back pocket on his way to the men's room, literally telegraphing his impending bowel movement. "Quit wasting time," he said. "We're so close to finishing the scene." But knowing that he probably needed this information more than anyone else, I picked up a dry-erase marker.

I told them to please be quiet. I congratulated them: "You guys are at the right place at the right time." I told them they were about to receive an early holiday gift; one that I'm sure even Santa Claus needs to hear. "Trim the beard, Kringle! Lighten up on the liquor, and stop hosting children on your elderly lap!"

Then I drew a picture of a vagina on the dry-erase board. Not the funny caricatures we'd all done on this same board for years. Not an animated *South Park*–style vagina with funny eyes and a country-western twang coming out of her sarcastic buck-toothed vagina-mouth.

I'm no artist, but I drew a crude rendering of what this thing really looks like; like I was inventing Braille for the blind, or a map for people who have never even heard of maps. I told these lucky men that what I was about to teach them would help them. Change things for them forever. That they should clear their cache of everything they ever thought they knew about pleasuring women. I began. I gave them step-by-step instructions on both the physical and the psychological levels of fucking ladies. A guy with too-curly black hair who went to Stanford dutifully took notes on his iPhone. I admired his courage in a roomful of professional mockers.

Later, when I opened the room up for questions, some asked specifics. You know the expression "there are no dumb questions"? ("Where does your pee come out?" "When you have your period, is it like a faucet that pours out blood?" "Why is the clit on the outside when my dick goes on the inside?") There totally are dumb questions, but I pretended otherwise. That particular writers' room usually greeted the dawn based on script deadlines. But this time, as the sun came up, these men walked into that new day fortified with something much more substantial than the hangover of poorly crafted puns.

A week later, there was a Christmas party for the show's cast and crew. Amidst the yuletide cheer and open bar, three of the writers' wives and two of their girlfriends approached me, thanking me for my frank lecture and tips. They were giggly and content, their men slightly swaggering. As I watched these couples connecting on a new level, I felt good. Proud to have been of service. And then I was suddenly overwhelmed by the thought of the many other men out there who also needed this information.

And that's why I'm here; why I'm compelled to tell this story. Not for the thanks—but because I never knew there was such a famine of knowledge. A fucking drought of well-fucked women.

I'm not digging wells to provide clean water to African children, but this is my charity. Women shouldn't need to be gay for their vaginas to be eaten properly. They shouldn't have to give detailed, emasculating instructions, either. This body of wisdom should be like the sacred Torah, passed down from generation to generation. Studied faithfully and practiced in earnest. I want to help you to pleasure your women in a way that many of you have no clue how to do. And why would you? How *could* you, if someone who owns a vagina doesn't offer some helpful hints and tricks?

While I was having sex with myself or other girls, you were masturbating at a speed that's the opposite of what's good for women. So I have an advantage, and it's time to share it.

You're trying to fuck a woman; I get it. I've done it. I aim to do it again in a couple of hours. But you've got to ask yourselves, "What's my goal here?" If you're just in this to put your penis in a vagina, there's plenty of alcohol and women with low self-esteem who will probably allow you to. But I would like to get you up and fucking, and to keep doing it until it actually feels like something more than just a sexual act; something like love.

This will require a new system.

Chapter 1

Learning How to Fuck Is Easier Than Learning How to Listen

"It won't work if I tell you what I want because if
I tell you what I want, I won't want it anymore."

I am convinced that there are only two types of men. Those who, when I tell them I'm writing a book on this topic, say, "Oooo, *I* should write that!" Or the other ones who say, "Oooo, when can I *read* that?" Please. Be the latter.

No, I'm not a man, but we do share things in common. We both love women. Okay, okay, we both love to fuck women.

MAJOR LIFE SPOILER ALERT: A man once said to me, his tongue thick with tequila, "Any higher degree I've earned, job I've gotten, language I've learned, jacket I've purchased, dinner I've paid for, vocabulary word I've flaunted, haircut I've received, compliment I've given, book I've read . . . Literally every action I've ever taken, is all in pursuit of pussy." This blew my mind. Still does, right now as I share it with you. His statement gave me so much insight into the mind of a man, so I approach all of this with his words in mind.

My mission here is altruistic. Men need to know how to care for and operate a woman. As a gay woman who moves invisibly between the genders, I feel like I have an obligation to help the world here. I'm like a delegate of the United Nations; I speak both languages, so I can pass information freely back and forth. What you do with that translation is up to you.

Men tend to confide in me, assuming that because I also love women, I'll feel the same way they do. They assume that I have the same interests they do. They talk about their shit with me like I have a sympathetic bro ear. They can share with me the dull ache of their loneliness at feeling misunderstood by their partner . . .

NO! Guys don't talk about things like that at all. If they feel something, they don't mention it. You men don't have time to, because you're in the pursuit of pussy. Your girlfriend's pussy. A stranger's. An ex's. Occasionally your wife's. A theoretical vagina. A fictional one. One that you once loved. One that you aspire to loving. Internet vagina. Vagina stills. Video. Audio sounds odd, but probably that, too. You even love the way a couch pillow can get all squished together in a vagina-seeming way. You love when a female yawns because you can see the entirety of her oral vagina. You can't help it. You get aroused watching a woman eat a banana.

You love it, and yet you don't want to talk about it, so every time a woman tries to process her emotions of feeling misunderstood or underappreciated, *you are not listening.* You are watching their sucking lips move; the lips that even have the same *name* as vagina lips. (This is no coincidence; the person who made up the word "lips" was undeniably some ancient dude with a boner.)

Men Are Hunters; Women Are Gatherers

Men are always in active forward movement. Or else they're asleep with a hand on their crotch. Men were once hunters, women once gatherers. We've all heard this in some anthropology class somewhere, or maybe a *Flintstones* cartoon. But women are still gatherers. Gatherers of boring feelings they need to discuss aloud with a gender that literally *could not give a shit.* They are feeling, talking, and crying—while you are almost rooting for her to sob, if only to see her tits start bobbing.

Of course, these are generalizations. There are exceptions, which is why some couples can make it work. If women can stop sharing feelings long enough to *be,* and men can stop *being* long enough to feel, a rare connection can bloom. Gather a few more of these moments, and you may have a love that endures. As a person who straddles the fence of having feelings while simultaneously being bored by them, believe me, I get it.

As you probably know, there are actual courses that claim that any man can get any woman if he simply sets his sights on them. That if you attend a seminar or pay for a series of costly DVDs, if you subscribe to a website or obtain an entirely new personality (which includes being confident and rich and handsome), you can fuck any girl in the world. Yes, you, too, can learn how to approach women. These books and sites offer the lines to use in any given scenario, and how to comport yourself to get pussy. You can memorize all the "best" pickup lines and learn from scummy guys how to allegedly treat women, right up until the moment you ejaculate.

> NEWS BLAST: Women who can be hooked with a line, or picked up with the tricks in these seminars, are generally not the women you want to have long-term relationships with. If you are not seeking a long-term relationship with a woman, that's perfectly fine—but then, there is no need to try to understand them. You may now return to your solitary takeout menus, online gaming, and looking around for an odd sock to ejaculate into.

Bartering: Trade Thoughtfulness for Sex

The first step in your quest to fuck a woman is trying to understand her. This is nearly impossible, because women are so goddamned unreasonable and hormonal and inconsistent. But they smell good and have boobs, so shut up and listen. I will break it down to an essential rule: in order to get, you have to give. Learn to trade being thoughtful for sex. It's like that little infinity symbol that keeps playing the music on iTunes. Those arrows in a tiny circle. If you share, you will receive.

You have heard this a million times. Golden Rule shit here: treat others as you want to be treated. Except your instincts are wrong. Your instincts have gotten you here, holding this book which feels nothing like a pussy, so let's assume you've made a couple of missteps along the way. You should do the opposite of your instincts. Let's call this the Reverse Golden Rule: treat others as they would want you to treat them.

An example. You would love it if she gave you a little space when you got home from work. If you have a god-damn job. (If you don't have a job, you've got bigger problems like unemployment, depression, and probably alcoholism.) But if you do have a job and therefore a boss, you're sick of his/her crap, always complaining and criticizing and expecting you to do work. If you are someone's boss, when you get home you want to be quiet and left alone. You want to unplug your brain that has been in output mode for the past eight to twelve hours. You want to stop thinking a few moves in advance, because you've been doing that all day.

But a woman requires this same type of strategic talk, and sometimes your brain needs a break. You compart-mentalize, and you need to put your brain on ice for a few minutes after you walk in the door. Unfortunately, this is in the same moment that she sees you, realizes that she has missed you, and wants to connect with you. This is horrible timing because you are decompressing from mental overuse.

However, your body feels available when she approaches you for this emotional connection. She is chopping out the overly detailed moves of her day, while the whole time you're thinking, "When, where, and how can I remove the semen from my ballsack?"

Women's Favorite Foreplay Is Being Listened To

But guys, this is shortsighted. If you want to fuck, you're going to have to go against your natural instincts. You must do the *opposite* of what you want to do, and that is to listen to her. Think of her need to engage. Her word emissions are a form of verbal ejaculation. It actually soothes women, untangles us. So, as we go through the wilds of our days—work slights, kids' fights, home mishaps—it is hard for us to move forward or even ask you about your day until we have monologued about our day. *Being listened to is our foreplay.*

This is so painful—I get that. It's a speed bump that you desperately want to blow past. But be generous now so that later on, you can be selfish. If women haven't had a chance to download, the last thing on their minds is fucking. But, if they come into a room and see that you are bent down and playing some idiot pretend game with your daughter, not only does she know that's one less thing she has to do, but she appreciates your thoughtfulness in putting your kid's needs first. And later, it may inspire her to put your needs first and possibly in her mouth.

Listen, I know you don't want to be running around wearing a princess crown and an old plastic lei, but it shows your woman that you are capable of thinking outside yourself, and that is what she's looking for. It is symbolic, and it will get you the results you desire. Once your desires are satisfied, you can resume being selfish for a finite period until you have the urge for sex again—which is certainly a finite period.

Don't Try to Fix

Here is the most important thing in understanding women, and therefore earning your ability to consistently fuck them. It is essential. The key to the vagina kingdom is: Don't fix. Just listen. This is so difficult, but it is so essential. Think of your penis not as a screwdriver, but as a microphone.

Yes, we like sex (actually, we love it!), but if we have bad feelings, you won't get laid. I know it's annoying, but we want to discuss our whole day with you. I call this "yammering out the details." It's trying to catch you up on the slights and intrigues of all the time that we're not with you. We think it will give you insight into our headspace. I get it; you don't care. But she won't get that, because this is an important part of her process. Just like blankly watching TV or sitting way too long on the toilet is an important part of yours. (What happens in there, anyway?) It pares down to you wanting to be left alone in your process, while women want to be heard and joined in ours.

Men don't want to listen; they want to fix. But women don't want your solutions. Yours never make sense to us. Your solutions annoy us. If you jump in and try to fix her "problem," things will heat up because she won't feel understood. So the quickest and best advice—hard as it is to actually do—is to shut your mouth.

We women feel about your ears the way you feel about our tits. Instead of your fixes for solving our problems, we want your empathy, and to know that you're listening. Conversely, you mostly just want us to be quiet. Here's a tip from way behind the enemy lines, some real gender Benedict Arnold shit here: you don't even have to listen. Of course it would be excellent if you did, but even if you just look at her attentively, you're already way ahead of the game.

Appear interested, undistracted. No TV, no computer, no texting. Even chewing is annoying. Don't floss, either. Let us blather. Nod occasionally. Try to avoid fidgeting. Focus. Take tiny breaths. Ask questions about details you could care less about. "Did she really say that?" "Was that after you went to the bathroom, or before?"

She'll talk endlessly about nothing you could ever possibly be interested in, sometimes very passionately. "I think she even flirts with the boss so her ideas get approved, which she would completely deny. But I don't think it's an accident she wore that skirt—it's not like she doesn't know she has nice legs—the same day the regional manager came to do her review."

Use These Words Sparingly

You fear that her speech and the other topics she so easily toggles to once she believes she has your attention will never end, but they will—when you use the following two words. I must encourage you to use them sparingly. If you use them too much, she will catch on. The key to ensuring sex later is speaking the following words right now: "I understand." When you've used this phrase a few times, it can become "I get it." Or even "I *so* get that."

These short word combinations are the key to it all. Gradually, they will even become true for you. You *will* understand, because even if you don't think and feel like she does, listening to her blather on will create that muscle for you. You're not a dog, you don't speak dog language, but over time, you have learned the nonverbal signals of your pet needing to go outside.

These two words, "I understand," also come in handy during a fight that you barely comprehend the reason for. Forget expensive flowers. Instead, use the words, "I understand," or the even far more rare and therefore treasured, "I'm sorry." You may worry that saying this will somehow weaken you, but in reality they make you and your relationship stronger. And you will get to fuck way more often.

Sex with No Strings Is a Myth

Another key to understanding women is that for many, a lot of her quest is about finding some version of a postmodern Prince Charming, however she may define that. I know it seems arcane, but let's assume one thing is true: for most women, sex is a means to an end. Sure, yes, an orgasm, but ultimately it is about an emotional connection.

Emotional connection after emotional connection equals happily ever after. Most of the time, you shouldn't believe her when she says she's only into it for the hookup. And, if she really did just want to have sex with you with nothing further expected, it's time to look at yourself. After all, if she only estimated you as a sport-fuck, this means she doesn't think of you as an appropriate lifetime partner. So, time to consider, what's missing in you if that's the only way she's willing to think about you?

Sex with no strings attached is almost as big a myth as Snow White and the Seven Dwarfs. Fairy-tale endings are tough to come by. There's a reason there were white horses and castles and disemboweling in those tales. It was the olden times. People shat outdoors. These stories were written with a feather quill. That's how antiquated the notion of happily ever after is.

Stories about seven little people—totally fine to call them dwarfs back then. One of whom, you may remember, was an actual medical doctor. Well, they thought it was a perfectly okay decision to stick an unconscious poisoned girl, who seemed to be dead (at the very least, time was of the essence), inside a glass coffin and wait for a stranger—a royal stranger, no less—to ride up in the desolate woods and wake her with a kiss. That was their solution.

What are the odds of a prince with a necrophilia fetish coming upon this particular scene just in the nick of time? That's weirder than anything even *Dateline* could come up with. Nowadays, even the dopiest and/or bashful of the little people would reach for his phone to ask Siri to find the poison control center: "Hey there, hi, this probably isn't on your list, but can you tell me what the antidote is for "poisoned apple"? No, I don't know if it's a Fuji or a Macintosh. It's red. Does that help?? A kiss? Seriously? Ohhh, a royal kiss. That makes way more sense. Thank you very much, operator."

Women get a bad rap for their unrealistic expectations, waiting for their knight in shining armor, their Prince Charming. But men want the equivalent, in a way. You want all your emotional and sexual needs met without ever having to discern them, articulate them, or do too much work to get them. Happily ever after without having to look up from your screens, sandwiches, or porn.

Snow White's only qualification for becoming Mrs. Charming is that she is the "fairest of them all." That's it; that's her whole thing. No one asks if she can cook a decent goose over an open flame, slash the neck of a charging wild boar in the dark heart of the forest, or pen a witty tweet. And the prince instantly falls in love with her without ever speaking to her at all. In fact, Snow White's dad, the King—the one who married the evil stepmother who conjured up all this drama in the first place—married this not-so-nice woman only because she was hot as shit. That stepmom was the preeminent hottie of the land until she took out an unsuccessful hit on her own stepchild(!). And Snow White's dad married this bitch, so look at the parental role model Snow had. Her dad prized beauty above all else.

Before the Queen was an evil stepmother, wasn't she probably an evil mean girl in general? Didn't she create a whole bunch of drama amongst the other girls in the kingdom? I assume she probably screwed over some of her best wenches in order to catch the King's attention. I'll bet that shit was epic. Lying, cheating, too much ale pong and deleting of royal texts. But it didn't matter to Snow's dad (who incidentally, kind of falls out of the story). He might've guessed it may not end well for his daughter. His only qualification for wife was "fairest in the land." It was like online dating, where women can spend hours and weeks filling out the wittiest, pithiest online question-naires, while men are just whizzing by, checking out who has the biggest tits or reddest lips.

All this is to say that often both genders place an unre-alistic amount of value on looks and appearances. I guess I can't really make the generalization as to which gender does this more, but it's men. No shit. Obviously, it's men. Not that women aren't guilty of this, too, but how often do you see a super-hot woman with a disgustingly obese or obscenely elderly man? Him: panting and sweaty on the bottom. Her: doing all the work before his congested, fatty arteries explode. (Do you have to imagine them making love? Or is this only me? I wish I could stop myself.)

Would the kiss of a commoner have awakened Snow White? Those dwarfs could feverishly dry-hump Snow White for hours (and of course they did)—why would anyone think she only cooked and made their little beds, washed and sewed and knitted for this gaggle of teeny men? For sure, Snow White spent the better part of her day relieving these seven dwarfs of their pesky dwarf semen. "Oy, I wish it were only six!" she must have muttered between dwarf BJs.

Quality versus Quantity

But either way, if the remedy for her poisoning is kissing, Snow White wasn't waking up from the kisses of their seven stubby little dicks. Let's face it: Snow White awoke from the dead because of the kiss of someone who owned a royal penis. You have to be Prince Charming. And no, you don't need to look like him, have his cool lineage, or even own an especially high-caliber steed. You just need to have his manners and his ability to listen.

Maybe you already *can* fuck anyone you want. And maybe this is the most important thing for you to be able to do. But doesn't it always run dry? I mean, sure, of course, you *can* pick up stupid women who fall for stupid pickup lines (which is what those seminars should really be called). But women, like anything else, can be more or less valuable based on their own self-esteem. Generally, the ladies who fall for the pickup lines taught at seminars are the women who can *be* picked up. The question is, do *you* want them?

If the answer is yes, that's okay; I get it. It means you value quantity over quality. So go ahead, keep fucking them until you're sick of it. If it feels great, keep on thrusting. You'll notice that even consummate bachelor George Clooney fucked many different people (however serial monogamously) until he was ready not to. But there was a point at which he liked and respected the person he was fucking enough to entertain fucking her for a lifetime. Even Clooney tapped out on fresh, new pussy.

Vaginas Are Like Snowflakes That You Can Fuck

I know. Most of you assume you totally know what you're doing, fucking-wise: "Hey, I got this." But women are the most complicated things on Earth, and they don't come with instruction manuals. Even if they did, you'd just throw them away. In fact, you wouldn't want anyone to see you buy this book, but you'll purchase endless lessons on the best golf swing. You'll explore websites with video game hints, tips, tricks, and secrets for hours. Even into adulthood, you read and memorize sports statistics; information you can't share with anyone who isn't in your own peer group. I know that I risk offending, but no fuckable female with a working vagina cares what Ken Griffey Jr.'s 1999 batting average was (.284, what does this even mean?!)—except maybe Ken Griffey Sr.'s wife. And, odds are, she probably won't have sex with you.

But you read, you memorize. You play sports, shooting basket after basket. You fail, you continue. You pore over porn. Maybe you're studying, researching thoughtfully, looking for new ways to please a woman—and then, uh-oh, physiology takes over. You get distracted by your erection, your investigation knocked down the priority list. Your sperm percolates like millions of microscopic popcorn kernels, no added trans fats necessary. If they could, your sperm would say, "Oh, please, help us escape, there's only so much room! It's so overcrowded in here, it's testicular sardines! How do we get out?!" And then you masturbate and come, and then close the computer window and delete your history, oh so sleepily. Every bit of investigative data forgotten, shot out along with your sperm.

Your research project over, sleep consumes you. "What was I looking up anyway . . . ?" Let's face it: sex is your engine, every single minute of every second of every day— and for that, you may not think you need any clues on how to operate the machinery. You're cool with guessing where this thing gets placed properly, or how to get the most pleasure out of the experience. You're fine with the skill set that you've been able to cobble together. You have to have, like, four hundred hours of experience to pilot a plane in the sky, but sex—*that* you're cool with.

As many ways and angles as there are to see vaginae on the computer, there's no substitute for seeing them up close and for real. As boys, when you first arrived at the site of your expedition, no one had prepped you as to what to do with it. And back then, you may not have even cared, because you just wanted to stick your penis in a hole and have some friction. At the end of the day, most boys are not picky eaters. However, now that you're a grown man and have dined out a bit more, maybe you're ready for more diversity of palate. Maybe you're ready to learn how to finesse your skills.

But up until now, who were you supposed to ask for advice? And if you did ever ask anyone—maybe when you were younger, or drunker—would they have had any clue? Did your college frat brothers know anything about pleasuring a woman? How could they? You never came up to them and tentatively wondered, "So listen, dude, I know there are drunk bitches passed out all over the urine- and sweat-stained couches, but what are their intrinsic emotional needs? How can I be sensitive to them in a culture obsessed with their appearance? And after answering that, will you give me a coupla tips on pussy eating? 'Cause, come on, that shit's fucking crazy."

When you were a teenager, did you think of asking your parents? Nah. Blech, they jammed their private areas together and made you. You came out of that hairy vagina (you know it is! Unless your mom is exceptionally young or slutty, her pubic region is an overgrown bush the width of a potholder). Now *she's* going to school you on how to fuck a vagina? Not very likely. Your dad? Ew. You were generated in his sweaty nut sack—those same saggy, crepey balls he's probably adjusting right this very second. You are the lottery winner, the lucky sperm that lived from the millions who died in Kleenex and toilets and sweat socks and rubbed away under the driver's seat of the car. Congratulations: you are the genetic appointee who avoided getting swallowed by your not-wanting-to-offend-but-not-super-down-with-it mother.

So who are you gonna ask? Oh, what about asking a female friend? As if there is such a thing. You'd never be that vulnerable with someone whom you could potentially enter. So whom do you ask? And moreover, whom do you rely on? ("Whom" is such a fancy word for this topic, isn't it? Like a crack whore wearing Chanel lipstick and a fancy church hat.) Because there's a lot of shitty information out there. The Internet, like the world, has many disgusting neighborhoods in it. There's nothing on there that will teach you sex the way they can teach you how to have a better golf swing in ten easy lessons. And golf, by the way—*that* you'll practice for hours. I once saw a guy practicing his swing using a doggie pooper-scooper in lieu of a sand wedge. But practice eating a vagina? He'd rather scoop the poop.

Let's be honest here: the vagina is an odd-looking thing. I get it, and I own one. And allow me to tell you from experience: no two are alike. Vaginas are skin snowflakes. Some have big outer lips, some have small inner labia; some have a lot of hair, some have no hair; some are wet, some are dry, some are thin and simple, some are chubby with complicated beefy reefs. (I feel as though I'm writing a pervy Dr. Seuss book.)

I mean, you must just be stunned when you get down there. Long or short, thick or thin, a penis is basically a hunk of skin with some oddities dangling off the bottom of it. (Hey, guys, your balls are totally as fucking weird and daunting as our vaginas. Big! Small! Droopy! High! Tight! Hairy! Saggy! Thing One and Thing Two!) But you are questing from puberty on to get to women's hole-y grail. One that you've only seen through endless porno portals that don't do this organ justice. You're dying to shake hands with this elusive epidermal Eden up close and personal. But when you finally arrive, ready to plant the flag, you must be confounded by its shape and differences from your own genitals. (A space alien upon seeing a vagina for the first time: "I know! It's a sweaty elk's ear! Oh, no, on Xytron we have something just like this! It's a hairy pile of prosciutto!")

So, yes, we women are different. Sure we're different from you physiologically—but we're also different from each other emotionally and mentally. Don't make assumptions about one and apply it to us all. You will irritate us, and when we're annoyed, we are also sexually stingy.

Women Have "Tells"

Observe and digest—as if you're sitting at a poker table and looking for "tells." Women have them, too. You will be patient at a table for hours, memorizing a furrowed brow or a quickened chip shuffle based on someone's poker hand, but you think that a woman is too boring to study for emotional tells even though the potential value of the pot can be far richer. So sit, listen, digest; and when you make a move, do it gently and with premeditation. It can win you a jackpot.

Be patient, even when she is bugging the hell out of you. No matter the extreme detail she needs to engage in, or the explication of what you perceive as irrelevant emotions—they are important to her. If you seem as if you are glazing over, she will be offended. Don't exclaim, "I'm so bored, why are you asking me to care about this?" or, "Can you tell this with way less detail? I don't give a shit what her uncle's cat's name is." Any version of this, no matter how true it feels for you, will hurt her feelings. Even if you can't understand why she needs to drag you through all this minutiae, admit defeat and just let her go on and on. Think about the Dow Jones, or the Häagen-Dazs bar you ate instead of lunch. Appearing to listen to her long, drawn-out story is what will eventually encourage this anecdote to end.

So act as if you're listening carefully, even ask an occasional question, as if you give a shit. She will be pleased that you're interested. It will benefit her in her discourse, and *you* in intercourse.

Chapter 2

Dating
Pretending to Be Someone You're Not

"I'd like a sorbet, and I'm fairly certain he'd like sex."

Look at yourself in a mirror. See not what you are familiar with ("That guy sure looks cozy!"), but the message that your physical presence sends. What does your "look" say about you? Snap judgments aren't always accurate, but nine times out of ten, they're an effective time-saving tool. It's the proverbial judging a book by its cover. If you're sloppy, lame, or out of it—or if you dress in keeping with the last year you had a great sexual run—chances are, you should shake it up a bit.

Just because loose, low-slung jeans worked when your last relationship began (around the same time University of Miami beat Nebraska in the Rose Bowl) doesn't mean they are still relevant. Keep up with the trends, even if you aren't setting them. Don't be overweight or overly colorful, and think in advance about those sleeves of tattoos. They are the same flappy arms that will play bridge and shuffleboard later in a retirement community. It's like we tell children: "Don't color on the couch. Ink is for paper." You can throw paper away after you've made a bad choice. As opposed to living the rest of your life with a Chinese symbol engraved into your forearm that translates to "Sweet and Sour Chicken." (A hilarious chuckle at twenty-three, but not really sure it stands the comedy test of *forever*.)

Create a Look

What if you don't have a "look"? How do you go about creating one? Check your age on your driver's license, because it actually matters. Then go out and buy one of those crappy gossip magazines, or go to a website with pictures of celebrities at various functions. Click past the weddings and formal award sections, and go to some daytime charity events. If you are young, you will look at what Drake or Zac Efron are wearing. If you are a few years older than that, you will see pictures of Hugh Jackman or Jay-Z on a step and repeat (the backdrop that advertises the charity event). Examine the clothes of your peer group. Do your clothes resemble anything they are wearing, stylewise? Does the cut of your pants seem similar; do the shades of their color palette seem vastly different? If so, follow these rules.

Go to your closet, or to your stuffed-to-the-max banged-up dresser that's as depressing as the clothes inside. If you haven't worn something in two years (most people say one, but you are thriftier and less eager to change than most), throw it out or give it away. If you have a cozy T-shirt that has sentimental value, give it to whomever you're fucking. It will make her feel special. She will want to wear it without panties to sleep in, or with her most beloved jeans to go get groceries.

If you are under thirty and not overweight, get skinnier jeans. If you are over forty, toss out those skinny jeans. Get rid of clothes that have tears, rips, or stains, unless you paid extra money for tears, rips, or stains. (However, please do not wear these types of age-embellished products after thirty-three. Thirty-three is when Jesus died, and I just can't picture him in distressed jeans.) It is okay to wear things besides jeans and T-shirts. Pants are not just for business meetings and funerals.

If you can afford it, invest in a good watch. If you can't, still wear a watch. Find your dead grandpa's old Timex and remove his yucky, broken Twist-O-Flex band. Attach a brand new twelve-dollar grosgrain band to it. It looks very cool. This says something about you: You have style, and a belief that time and something outside of yourself matters. Or that a grandparent once loved you enough to bequeath his cheap heirloom to you. Wearing a watch implies that you have responsibilities in life. You have to be places. I know, I know, it feels weird. It feels uncomfortable, and it constrains all that yucky hair that grows on your wrist. I know that you can always look at your phone to ascertain the time, but there is something handsome/ adult/post-collegiate about wearing a watch. It's a rite of passage—as if your arm had a bar mitzvah.

Regarding clothes, confine patterns to the small. If you are chubby, don't confuse your bloatedness with getting older. You need to go to the gym. The reason you stayed more slender when you were a kid was—yes, your metabolism was faster, but also because a bossy asshole wearing a comb-over and a generic-brand polo shirt was blowing a whistle at you in gym class for fifty minutes a day. Fact: if you ran around for fifty minutes every day now, you'd be way skinnier. Do not ignore your body, because it will respond by turning on you and becoming a piggy blob. It's tough to be motivated to want to fuck someone who seems not to care about himself enough to take care of his body. Your wife will do it with you sometimes, but she won't really be that into it. She will not make that extra effort or go out of her way (e.g., ball-licking) if you don't (e.g., running on the treadmill).

These rules are different if you both started out large, and/or loved each other into largeness. However, if this was a gradual or sudden shift to your current size, then initially you unfairly represented the package. Also, atrophied butter-soaked arteries are even more alarming. Because I can guarantee you that 100 percent of the time, you will always fuck better if your heart is still beating.

If you want to fuck someone who is physically pretty, lithe, and taut, yet you want to remain very corpulent or unattractive, the only way to do this successfully is to be frighteningly rich. If you are very rich and fucking someone who's extra hot, and you think she's fucking you because you are hilarious or inventive or witty, please know that she is only fucking you because you're smart enough to have figured out how to get all that money. But she's also fucking you because she's into the lifestyle: the private jet and the ice-encrusted watch and the nice person whose job it is to live in your home and make things easier for the owner. You know, the lady who prepares your woman a grilled cheese sandwich and tomato soup in the middle of the night because she's a little sad about something her dog said. I'm not judging, either. I'm proud of you for figuring out how to have it all, but please don't mistake her wanting your thick wallet with wanting your thick body.

Never stop evaluating yourself. Don't stop growing or changing in our ever-evolving world. Don't be afraid to ask yourself those very tough questions. My friend Josh's goatee looked like an unkempt mouth vagina. I explained to him that it's rare to find a woman who wants to kiss something like that. I told him that goatees are the facial hair equivalent of trench coats. The bearer always has something to hide. Weak chin. Assassin. On the lam. Gender transitioning.

Josh, bless him, was open to my advice. He shaved his hairy pussy-mouth, and suddenly an entirely different caliber of woman opened up for him. Turned out, his face bush was originally borne of shame; he'd grown it in college to cover up french fry acne that he'd contracted while smoking bales of marijuana. Without his mom there to nag him to eat right, stop smoking, shave his face, Josh got used to hiding behind his hair burka. Shaving it allowed him to stop hiding, like taking off a cartoon disguise. Can you imagine how much more ass Groucho Marx would've gotten if he'd shaved his 'stash and removed those glasses? I mean, not literally, because those women probably did want to fuck Groucho Marx—but you know what I mean.

Ask Questions, and Remember the Answers

Now that you're finally wearing pants and your face is free of antiquated facial hair, maybe you've made active plans with an adult female. You are sitting upright in a place that serves food. There is a napkin on your lap. On this first date, please pay attention to the small details. Ask questions and listen to the answers as if you're a grizzled TV detective gathering clues. Especially at the beginning.

Ask tiny interrogatory things that are seemingly unmeaningful: "Girl person, what is your favorite color?" Do not black out while she answers, as this will be on the test. "What is your favorite restaurant?" "What is your favorite type of See's chocolate?" All these tiny preschool preferences, a whole bunch of nonimperative nothings, will blend together into a delicious batter. She will even forget that she told you whatever her answers may be. For her, it's so much blather that will blend into a comforting ambient experience (the white noise of pleasantries) like, "Ooooh, that was a fun date." (She talked and talked, you listened and listened.) This will have her under your spell. Then, pocket her answers. Stow them away for later. Don't forget that fucking is a motherfucking complicated business. It's not checkers; it is *chess*—and you have to plan a few moves ahead.

If you are still interested in sticking your private area into her private area, but it hasn't yet occurred, ask her out again. Try recalling her answers to your banal questions. Remember that the sum of these answers will work to your advantage. Take her to her favorite restaurant that she will barely remember having mentioned. (Ooh, mind-reader!) Produce the box of chocolates with her favorite color of ribbon tied around it. (Ooooh, the little things!) Make sure that inside the box, there are only her hand-picked favorites. Just a pound of the kind she specifically mentioned; e.g., milk-chocolate almond caramels. No random and prewrapped package like the kind you grab at an airport kiosk. No annoying cherry goops or marsh-mallow splats or dark chocolate jellies to tentatively bite halfway into and discard, annoyed to have wasted calories on anything less than perfection. Just the ones she loves and said aloud, and that you *remembered*. For you, it was annoying to listen to, and irritating to go out and buy. (Why the fuck does it matter? Who cares about a bunch of stupid candies? Won't she be mad at me for giving her chocolate because she'll complain about her weight? Is this the 1950s?)

Whoa, whoa, whoa. It isn't *really* about the chocolates, dumbass. You can apply this same "listening" to any kind-ness. It makes her feel globally heard and meaningfully remembered. She has the concrete evidence that you listened, processed the information, and thought about her when she wasn't there. Which is *everything* to her. And you will most probably get your penis sucked for this relatively cheap gesture—which is everything to *you*. So, in actuality, listening is very selfish.

Manners: have them. I know they may seem arcane, a nod to a time long ago before you could download etiquette apps for $0.99. It's all the stuff your grandma nagged you about, right? "Hold a door open for a woman." "Get out of the car to open her door." "Pull out her chair at a table." "Get up when a lady enters." "Walk her to her door." "Offer her your coat." "Carry her purchases." "Pay for her shit." "Offer her cunnilingus." All this stuff. But just knowing how to properly use a knife and fork goes on her checklist; she sees that manners were important in your family. So this is a nod to history and education. You don't need to open a door for a woman or pull out her chair. But it is a paean to a time lost, and—if you're interested in sucking on her titties—it is something women notice when you *don't* do it more than if you do. So make it seem effortless, like you do this annoying shit all the time.

In terms of sexual manners, Emily Post may never have typed on her typewriter: "Gentlemen, do not hasten to blast a surprise load upon a young lady's face, catching her unawares your first time up at bat." But perhaps that was based on her own lack of firsthand experience. Her suitors were probably too afraid their ejaculate would glob together in the feathers of one of her ornate hats, so they naturally shied away from this activity.

Dating Is the Best It Will Ever Get

So, what to do on a date? First of all, in these modern times, make one. Actually pick a time, place, and location. Put it in your iCal. Where to go? Who cares? Look, it's all a silly charade meant to test the waters. You are both mutually temperature-taking to see if there's sexual chemistry, so it's all a bit false, anyway.

In fact, it's a goddamn show. It's practically a Broadway musical, with makeup and hair, costumes and sets. Acting like you're someone you're not, to gain a stranger's approval. She actually applied hot wax to her labia and had it ripped off so that you might be visually pleased. This is not what real life looks like. After she has had three of your kids, she's just gonna try to whack away at that shit with a cheap five-pack pink drug-store razor, and hope you're not looking too closely during your seven-minute shove-in. This dating time is the best it's ever going to get, so if you're not into her now, you're never going to be.

You might think you'll know within a few minutes whether this person is right for you. No! Stop. You may be blowing the opportunity of a lifetime. Just wait a few beats longer than you ordinarily might before making your final judgment. Humans are, by nature, reactive. It's fair to say that you can't really judge anyone on a first date—even though you will and do. She is struggling to impress you, and she is absolutely not herself. She is the best version of herself based on a guess she makes about what *you want her to be*. But don't blame her: *you are not yourself, either*. You are a superstar boring-anecdote listener, a nonfarter, a new-shirt wearer, a napkin dauber. So let's just hold off judgment until date number two, or at least the latter part of this one.

Always offer to pick her up. Don't be offended if she won't allow you to, due to her fear that you're a Ted Bundy type. Men are usually bigger physically, so if she says no to your stopping by her place, it's either because you're still a stranger, or she wants to be in control. As in, she may want to ditch you in case you're a loser. (Still, she wants you to *ask* her if she wants to be picked up, because that confirms the dateyness.)

Defy the Odds: Ask Her about Her

Be a reporter on date one. Ask questions. Pretend to listen. Have follow-up questions. Do an 80:20 ratio in terms of asking things about her, versus discussing yourself—even though we know that you are way more interesting to you than she is. Don't just wait to start talking. She has the same feeling in reverse, and is so excited that you seemingly defy the odds of most men only being interested in themselves. So ask questions, and let her speak. If she's boring, watch her lips move. Look at her boobs bounce when she's saying something emphatic. See? This isn't so hard. You can do it! Reward yourself by asking another question. Oh, wait—maybe something she says actually relates to you and your life. You identify with something she's said. Avoid making this analogy out loud; you can always share that kinship later. And, if you bring it up later, it will seem like you have given some thought to what she's had to say.

You do want her to get to know you, but let's face it: the real you doesn't have these upright, interactive, face-to-face conversations very often, so think of this as showing off. Your focused attention will make her feel appreciated, and show her your capacity for listening. She will attribute a personality to you that you don't really have, and potentially reward your imaginary self with real-life lovemaking.

In choosing where to go on this date, pick somewhere you've gone before. Know the lay of the land, but DO NOT associate this place with another female. I know you believe that memories don't bug you, but they are like an air-conditioning filter. They clog the new, cleaner memories, congesting the current atmosphere. Another rule is to take her somewhere she'd never go by herself. Be clever, but by no means *too* clever. Don't go somewhere so odd that she will be afraid you're a psycho. A picnic in the desert may seem romantic to you because *you* know you won't kill her and bury the body, but she doesn't know that yet.

Please know her well enough, at this point, through texting or phone chats, to take into account what *she* may want to do. Don't take a recovering alcoholic to a wine tasting. Don't take someone with a nut allergy to a cooking class. Don't take a quadriplegic go-karting. Don't take a Jew to a luau. Invent one of your own here. Know your person well enough to know what would be an idiotic thing to do. The rule for date number one is: Be all about her.

On the second date, show her a unique aspect of yourself. Let her in on a secret. Do you love scouting for vintage T-shirts at thrift stores? Do you go to the observatory to check out the constellations? Do you like an out-of-the-way taco stand that only a few people have heard about? If you get to the second date, go somewhere that shows a side of you that may feel surprising to her. Hey, no shit, but it doesn't have to be real. Take her somewhere that reveals a quality or interest you *wish* you had. Obviously, it's better if it's the real you. But if it's more intriguing if the revelatory thing is that you like to volunteer at a children's hospital or you like to pick up trash on the beach, go for it. It will improve your chances of getting to the fucking.

But also keep in mind that it could backfire. You may have met your forever match, and now you will be stuck with a lifetime of ladling thin stew for the homeless. So, if you intend to proceed with this relationship as anything more than just the physical, search for something about yourself that's emotionally revelatory. Bowl if you must, but know that it requires women to lift heavy things, type numbers, and wear used shoes. Your chances of getting it in will go way down.

Date Three Is for Fucking

Historically, date three is for fucking. Set up some kind of cursory activity before you get to the real reason for the date. Caution: don't take her for Indian or Thai food, or anything too gastronomically complicated. Spice produces gas. Gas produces inhibition, shame, and fear. The odds of fucking exponentially decrease if she is experiencing curry bloat. (This may not apply if she is actually Indian. Her system may be slightly more inured.) Just try to keep it simple on the first potential fuck date. If you have already fucked on dates one and/or two, congratulations and skip this section.

But if you haven't . . . no spicy. Change the sheets. Empty the trash. I know that may not sound important, but the contents of the wastebasket in your bathroom are a literal evidence locker; a catch-all, a clue giver of what's occurred in your home recently. Used golden waxed Q-Tips? Blech. Blood? Oh no! Used condoms? All way too much information. She will go to your bathroom and she will snoop, I promise. She won't poke around long enough for you to think she may be doing a number two in there, but she *will* scan and memorize.

If anything is too embarrassing, be aware of it enough to hide it. Think a couple steps in advance, because she does. Look at your bathroom, your bedroom, the contents of your fridge with her eyes. What does your Goober Grape Smucker's PB & J say about you as an adult man? What about your Rite Aid–purchased clamp light? What does your bedside reading material say? *Is* there any?

Look, if you want to increase your fuck chances, load up on your assets. The things you can control. Be the man you want her to *think* you are. Buy nice thread-count sheets. Clean the floors of shed hair or recently deceased spermatozoa. Maybe even add a chic costly candle with a scent that's not too overpowering. Something in the woodsy family. It shows you care about yourself enough to spend a little cash on the olfactory components of your life. Don't burn it way down, as she will think you're fucking a lot of girls. Don't do its white-wicked virgin lighting in front of her, either. It will be as if you bought it for the occasion.

I know you don't notice all these clues, but, as I mentioned before, *she* does. All of her friends know that she is out with you. They are waiting for a written report. Texts will come in soon. "How was it?" "Where r u?" "Omigod, are you still with him?" "Are you fucking right now?!" No matter what happens, she will go back to her friends and give a briefing. So make sure there is something extraordinary to report: "He has a monster cock!" Or even, "He had fresh grapes!"

As I've mentioned, everything matters; everything is calibrated, gauged, and analyzed. If you use an exclamation point or ellipses in a text, she will show this to a jury of her friends to ask what your intention was. "Why did he type these three dots . . .?" They will come up with a verdict, even if your intention was nothing. (Of course, it's nothing! Maybe you just had an especially good fart when you typed in those magical ellipses.) But that doesn't matter. She will already be treating you as if you have whatever ellipses disease her friends have diagnosed you with.

Women Like a Little Throw-down

Yes, yes, sure, always ask her what she likes to eat at a restaurant. Chat about the menu together: "What looks good to you . . .?" But then, when the server approaches, order for the table. ("Wait, Ali. Really? Don't women think this is presumptuous, antiquated . . . sexist?" Of course it is. But if you have a general sense of what she likes, then *this action imitates what you will do in the bedroom later*.)

So pull out her chair for her, but also know her well enough to order for her. Remember what she likes to drink. Don't even bother to ask; just do it. I will drink something with crème de menthe in it just because someone made an effort to take care of me and intuit my order. We all want to feel like there's a guiding and protective hand on the small of our backs. If you can help a woman feel this way, do it, because it is your surest road to fucking. Women like to have a little throw-down, a little take-charge-type bossiness. This makes her feel taken care of, and lets her know you are the man.

She likes it when you're the man, because it allows her to feel like a woman. This is most especially true if she is someone who is bossy in life and work. She likes to feel out of control a little at the table, and she especially likes this if it's a foreshadowing of the bedroom. Generally speaking, the bedroom is where she likes to hand over the reins. She will be jostled and jarred by your confident move (and kind of impressed: "Oooh, he's _that_ guy"). Men that mince around, or think they're being sensitive when they tell her to "Get what you want," will lose out. (Or the worst: "Go ahead and order for both of us.")

You think you're being respectful by letting her decide. But this just tells women that you don't know what you want in Thai food, or in life. It's a window into the bedroom; a snapshot of how you will be. It says that you are an abdicator. You will be tentative and ignorant in bed, and now she knows what to expect there. It's a goddamn microcosm. But if you come in with your dinner order, swashbuckler style, even if it's all wrong, she will at least appreciate that you gave her a little throw-down. _Having someone order for us tells us you know what you're doing._

You are steering the ship, and that lets a woman relax. She can do other things, like see if you smell good. If you help her in removing all of her control mechanisms, she can occupy herself with doing other things like thinking about kissing you. Your job in the prefucking period is basically to remove any of her doubts. She is skeptical of you, yet she is here with you—so she definitely wants to be proven wrong.

Some of this is her own insecurity: "Why is a seemingly normal person into _me_?" "He likes me enough to buy me food and make time for me. Doesn't he see that I'm a fraud and a mess?" "How can he be normal and single?" "Is he a player?" "Is this an act?" Everything is a sign during these early times, so we make neurotic general assessments. One too many drinks means he's an alcoholic. Being impatient in traffic means he will hit your future children. All we have to go on are these signals, so rein your shit in and be cool.

Okay, when ordering for the girl, a couple of obvious things. Don't order a dish that expressly lists garlic as an ingredient, or your breath will reek. If there are trace amounts of garlic in your food, use a mint. Seriously. We remember the song playing, the potpourri scent in the restaurant bathroom, the pants you selected; and when you kiss us, if you taste like a meal we didn't actually eat firsthand, we will note this forever. It will be far bigger than you ever intended. It will become part of the *legend*: "When Daddy kissed me for the first time, he'd just had a giant bowl of garlicky bouillabaisse." Or part of the *lore*: "Ugh, when that asshole kissed me, his mouth stank like a Sicilian's garbage pail." "Why would he order garlic?" "Didn't he *want* to kiss me? And if he did want to kiss me and he still ordered like that, it means he didn't think about my feelings at all. His needs are more important than mine, which will totally be true in a relationship with him, too—so fuck him! I'm not texting him back at all! In fact, I'm deleting his number." This shit really happens, I'm telling you, so the momentary bliss of buttery, crusty garlic bread maybe isn't worth the trade-off of a lifetime together.

Please. This is so important: *Don't talk too much about your ex or exes*. Be vague about your dating history. Promise yourself not to mention a girl's name unless your date asks very specifically about your recent dating history. Even then, keep it to fewer than fifteen (positive) words. Even if your ex gave a hand job to your best friend with the finger that wears the very expensive ring you bought for her. I know it's the hardest thing in the world, but only say kind things. *Just lie!* "She was a great girl. (She is a whore.) Didn't work out. (She is a liar.) We ultimately weren't right for each other. (Human Papilloma Virus.) And then, "I just want to talk about *you* tonight. Tell me about your favorite things to do . . ."

Just know that when she asks about your ex-history, she is not asking about your past; not really. She's asking about her (own) future. Will you trash her if it doesn't work out with you two? Will you obsess about her on a date with someone else? She wants to know that you are capable of having a relationship of some kind, so she doesn't need to teach you all the relationship primer tricks that I will cover in the next chapter. Look, I know you just want to get to the fucking, but you'll never get to do it if you don't settle down and listen up to all this other shit.

Chapter 3

How to Pick the Perfect Peach

DONNELLY

*"Nothing could be better than being here right now with you,
except, possibly, being right over there now with her."*

There isn't one way to catch a fish, but if you keep your line loose, whatever way the fish jumps and bends, you can eventually catch one. You must learn how, or you will go hungry. And finding women to fuck is like fishing. We women are mercurial motherfuckers, but it's not our fault. Women instinctively bob and weave. They are naysayers by nature, and they're difficult to read: Will she bite? Will she sneakily steal bait and swim quickly in the other direction? In this chapter, I'm going to show you how to make sure the vagina you're fishing for is the one that you really want to bite your hook.

There are all kinds of different fish in the sea, as your boring aunt used to say before her embolism. And you need to be able to distinguish what type of carp or cod or piranha you're trying so hard to reel in. Be aware and beware of the quiet ones; they're thinking things way too loudly inside. Beware of the noisy or bossy ones, too; they're often covering a tender or too-sensitive heart.

Beware of the too-skinny ones because they're not emo-tionally fortified either; the only things they eat are feelings of self-doubt and insecurity. And beware of the overly large; they're hiding shit like deep-fried emotions.

Diagnose What She Is Lacking

Women are all different, there is no hard and fast rule for seducing any specific one, but they all tend to telegraph what it is they need you to focus on. She is giving you all the clues the first time you see her. Just pay attention to her style choices and the things she says out loud. If you come across someone who is driven by appearances, spend time complimenting her. She's invested a lot of time and money on this for a reason; she wants her physical beauty acknowl-edged. But don't get suckered in by the superficial, just because she is. Go for the more subtle compliment. Get to the heart of the disease, not the cosmetic symptom. Like, if she's wearing heels, instead of just talking about her sexy red-bottomed shoes, compliment the attribute she's been compensating for with them. "You walk with such confi-dence. It's hot." *She didn't even know she needed to hear this.* Now you're a mind reader, and have added a sexual charge to your interaction. Mazel tov.

If she is a braggy-about-her-accomplishments type, this means that she hasn't been acknowledged by someone she respected. Go out of your way to be impressed with the thing she's leaving off the list. "How did you manage to earn a bronze medal in competitive swimming while still staying so close to your little brother? I'll bet he's grateful to have a role model like you."

Women who have a lot of friends are uncomfortable being alone, and need a jury to poll about their daily problems. Try to be available for time-consuming listening, and become an ersatz therapist. Go back and reread chapter 1.

Women who went to fancy colleges succeeded very early on in their lives. It wasn't accidental: they worked very hard; they are smart and test well. They still may like to boast about what they got on their SATs or replay tedious college anecdotes, long after graduation. But this is their backstory; these women studied and prepared while their less-impressive-college-bound peers were getting finger-fucked at the theater by butter-flavored digits. In order to stop her loop of nonhilarious collegiate reminiscences, replace her memories with something that is actually happening today. Show her the things she missed out on. Offer up some time-wasting college-type fun. Take her indoor sky-diving or, if she's up for it, shove a Twizzler inside her at the movies.

It's so simple; you must provide the antithesis to who she is, to promote her balance. Read her well enough to diagnose what she's lacking.

Let's say you're in a club and trying to get a woman's attention, but she's constantly looking around or focused on her phone. Try to get her to engage with you. If she won't, it means she's probably not available to you. Risk saying something potentially idiotic and vulnerable here. "Are you looking for someone who isn't me?" If she laughs, or opens up, you have a shot. If she avoids or confirms that it is not you, move on.

Don't set your sights on someone who is going to reject you. Even if you move forward to the next level, she will ultimately reject you. Don't want this for yourself just because your mom worked too much or your dad was absent. You should want someone who is available to you. Want someone whom you could love, and who could love you. Even if that doesn't happen tonight, and you just end up buying this girl and all her greedy friends too many drinks.

I asked a bunch of single guys to pick a few words to describe what they were looking for in a potential future lifetime partner. Here is a random sampling of their responses:

- Fun.
- Cute.
- Long hair!
- Hot.
- Not a slut.
- Trustworthy. (Sort of like not-a-slut.)
- Content. (This is about him, not her.)
- Good companion. (Again, about him. Not her.)
- Agreeable. (Implies that she agrees with him, so not really about her.)
- Likes my friends. (Call this a mirror; it reflects him.)
- Marriage material. (Nebulous at best.)

- Regular sex.
- Thinks I'm funny. (Alert: anyone who says this, is not.)
- Blond. (A super-purchasable goal.)
- Amazing cleavage. (This means fake boobs, or cleavage from real-life big boobs. You may not yet appreciate the smaller ones until later on in life. You may not understand the literal gravity of what you're asking for with big boobs. The large, natural breasts of a twenty-year-old are undoubtedly fantastic, but later on, and especially after kids, they are heavy, south-pointing sacks of sand. It's pay now, or pay later.)
- Good body.
- Thin. (Not necessarily the same as "good body," by the way.)
- Pretty face.
- Thin, pretty face.

Well, you get it.

Of the women I surveyed, sure, a lot of them said hot or handsome or sexy, but ALL of them said smart, funny, gets me. No one said ugly. No one said dumb. No one said smelly or gassy or quick to hit. So I guess that broke down pretty much the same across the gender lines. Now, blond is great for a night. Even twelve. A good physique is helpful, for sure. But does that seem like enough? Do men realize that eventually these qualities fall apart over a lifetime? Big picture: these thin, pretty characteristics may not hold up.

"Believe me, I've tried. There are just no good girls out there." I hear this all the time from guys. For whatever reason, he is usually Irish, and he insists that his penis is the exception to that stereotype about Irish men's penises. In every pile of married men I work or hang out with, there's always one lone holdout. A guy who, despite his true age, is perennially twenty-two in his thinking and actions. He judges his drone-ish married peers (those guys who got married and had kids in their twenties, thus following the Habitrail factory of life), while they live vicariously through him. They imagine his penis as their own (in the least gay way possible) as it thrusts around like a dog under a table looking for scraps, taking the internal temperature of the local vaginas. But every time this guy shares a new sexual adventure, he's always surprised that his choices aren't working out. Does he not get that he's the reoccurring character in all of his stories? His inability to recognize the right type of woman is the reason his stories don't wind up with a happily ever after.

My parents are divorced. My dad is happily remarried to the greatest woman in the world. I asked my dad, many years ago, when he was still married to my cheating mother, what qualities he was looking for in a wife *before* marrying my mom. (They got engaged on date number four—family lore. A Wednesday first date, Thursday date, Friday date, Saturday engaged. Technically, the marriage lasted twenty-two years.) Dad pulled a weathered-looking scrap of paper out of his wallet. Bet he'd looked at it a lot, blinking back just how wrong he'd been. Here's what it said.

My Wife in no special order:

1. Has a great personality.
2. Is physically attractive.
3. Is into me and loves me.
4. Is Jewish. (His family was killed in the war, so I get this. Propagate!)
5. Is intelligent. (Good for him!)
6. Is good in bed. (Blech!)
7. Wants children (Hey! That's meeee!)

It's a good thing he didn't mention a sense of humor, because my mom's is about as plentiful as water in California. He said that ten items on a list is very good, but no one person ever really gets more than seven, and my mom had seven.

I thought my dad was very pragmatic. I didn't press him about number six, which made me bilious to consider what his standards for sex may be. After all, how would he have gauged this? A cracked-toothed, thick-bellied, hand-rolled-cigarette-reeking Hungarian sixteen-year-old baby-sitter stole his virginity when he was six. That's right, *six*. When I declared what happened to him was molestation, my father, an actual medical doctor, a psychiatrist in fact, gave a lurid smile: "If that is molestation, then *molest* me!" he merrily decried. Not a trace of being victimized anywhere in him. That may sum up a lot of the entire male/female divide. My dad was thrilled to have a leathery-skinned, Slivovitz-stinking teenager grab his tiny ("Relax,

Dad, I'm sure it's very big now. You were six!") penis and scoot it into the vicinity of her giant banged-out opening. I'm sure if he heard that a male babysitter that he procured for me at six (he didn't trouble himself with this level of child-rearing detail, but let's just suppose . . .) had taken my virginity, he would begin looking for this man with a dull axe in one hand, a phone book in the other. He doesn't really get that the Internet may help in his murderous revenge quest. Point being, that what in hindsight plays out as a delightful sexual experience for Dad, when a fucked-up teenager steals his six-year-old innocence, would never be confusing to him for a six-year-old girl, especially his daughter. But his position wasn't as rare as you may think. All the guys in every room I've been in wished they'd had Mary Kay Letourneau as their teacher. (Crazy, crazy fact here. Mary Kay is still MARRIED to her victim/student/now-husband/baby-daddy.)

Okay, but back to Dad's list. So when looking for his wife number two, I wondered what qualities, if any, had changed for his particular search engine. He indulged me.

My Wife #2: (Again, in no special order.)

8. Has above qualities #1 through #6.

The new traits (assuming he learned some hard lessons over the course of his first marriage) for the revised list include:

9. Is an "actualized" person (i.e., is a grown-up).
10. Does not want to have a second family with me. (Phew! Avoidance of less attention and having to divide eventual, hopeful inheritance.)
11. Has her own career. (Nephrology!)
12. Is independent financially. (Be a nephrologist. You never go out of business!)

We Are Wired to Recreate Our Childhoods

Dad's list for wife number two was very fair. He learned something from his first wife: what *not* to do. So pretend you've already divorced your first spouse. The one who represents everything you didn't receive in your childhood. It's pathetic that we're so crudely wired to recreate our childhoods. Men and women can unite in this common bond. Childhood demons don't check for gender; we look for in our partners either what we did, or didn't, receive as kids. We recreate that blueprint, however glorious or fucked up. It is not purposeful; it is passive. This repetition is engrained. When a guy is looking for the impossible-to-find, the too-hot, the emotionally absent woman—sorry, but it is the combination of whatever he experienced as a child, most usually with his mom. Sometimes he will seek to correct this wound, and look for the opposite of what he received. That usually works out better.

So how do we *not* fall for the wrong person? How do we not pick the person who is most familiar to us? The one who emulates our most influential parent? Recreates the familiarity (and the fissure) of all that was wrong (or right) in our childhood home lives? We choose either who our parents were, or who they weren't. It's a crapshoot of familiarity and overcompensation for what we lacked. We basically pick what we know, until we don't need to pick it anymore. We make the same mistakes, attract the same basic person and have the same fights, until we're ready not to. Our childhood will always dictate our choices.

If you're fucking up your life by constantly picking the wrong women, it means your picker is off. Don't panic if you've got a shitty picker. To fix the picker, it's like learning anything; like how to toss a football or make a layup or some other sports-related analogy. It's not going to be easy, but I'm going to take the guessing out of it for you. I've baked up a few simple rules for you to follow until your picker gets stronger and more reliable, and you are able to choose on your own.

Ali's Rules for Who Not to Date

1. Don't date actresses or models. (Nothing in the "I need applause or adoration/love me, Daddy" field of employ.)
2. Don't date bisexuals. (Too complicated until your picker is more finely tuned.)
3. Don't date someone way smarter than you. Or the reciprocal: don't date someone way dumber.
4. Don't date the unemployed.

5. Don't date someone much younger or older than you. (Seven years max in either direction.)
6. No drug addicts or nonrecovering alcoholics. (You *will* want to fuck these people. Just don't.)

Other possible types to avoid:

- The woman who is overly attached to her mom or dad
- The woman who doesn't have a good relationship with her mom or dad
- The one who compares you to others
- The one who compares herself to others
- The criticizer
- The people-pleaser
- The man-basher
- The woman-hater
- The emotionally unavailable ones
- The one whose emotions are too readily available
- The too-mean woman
- The too-nice woman
- The takes-herself-too-seriously woman
- The one who doesn't take herself seriously enough
- The woman who has it all
- The woman who has nothing
- The too-flirtatious woman

- The woman who doesn't have any clue how to flirt
- The too-clingy
- The too-independent
- The woman who has done it all
- The woman who hasn't done enough . . .

Well, you get it. Don't date in the extremes.

As you get better at picking women, these rules can lighten up, but for now, just color inside the lines. Plenty of time for freehand later.

I get it. Guys say what women want to hear until you really get to know them. For guys, vaginas literally say what they want to hear: Nothing.

The Vagina Effect

The vagina is a most alluring creature. For men, the feeling of penis in vagina supersedes all reason. Rational behavior occurs only in hindsight. We only see why our relationships end, after the fact. But ask any of our clear-eyed friends, those unaffected by the druggy effects of genital mind-poisoning; they will have a long, cogent list of the reasons why it didn't work out for you. Real obvious shit, too. Ten Commandment–style stuff. Lying, cheating, stealing, coveting . . . but in the initial pussy-drunk phase where your physiology (due to adrenaline) actually changes, you can't see anything with clarity. This isn't the same thing as "beer goggles," where your standards are clouded because you're inebriated. This is the "Vagina Effect." Once in, we can convince ourselves that someone is something they are not. It can also be referred to as "Cock Hypnosis." But that seems way more crass.

For the man who has a tough time making sound choices, certain types of women should be tagged with warnings akin to those on packs of cigarettes. Avoid these, please. At least until your picker improves.

CAUTION: This type of woman may be hazardous to your emotional health.

CAUTION: This type of woman may be addictive.

CAUTION: Quitting this type of woman greatly reduces serious risks to your feelings.

Some groups to potentially avoid:

1. Don't date actresses or models.

Actresses and models are people who pretend to be something else for a living. These performers went into this industry because they either need people to literally applaud them, or to chronically remark upon their talent and/or physical beauty.

Years ago, I was in a writers' room with a guy who mused, "Yeah, you know, I'd still fuck Farrah Fawcett." Oh wow, I'll bet Farrah, who was then still very much alive, would've lit up to hear that a chubby Jewish kid from Pittsburgh, who was already making do with a third of his hair in his early thirties, "still" would've fucked her. I used to catch this guy, this Adam or Josh or Eric (none of these are his name, but oh so close), picking his nose behind his doodled-on TV script, thinking he'd built a successful paper screen to shield us from his grossness. I wondered about his word choice: "still." This nebbish who masturbated to Farrah's poster at least as many times as the twenty million copies it sold (are posters still a thing?) claims that he'd "still" fuck her. Why "still"? I guess because she was in her early fifties by then. Still unshakably gorgeous. Can you imagine if someone ran up to her mid–crab cake bite at the Ivy at the Shore with the news that, despite her advanced age, a portly nose-picker who chronically pitched cat names as jokes ("Mr. McFluffypants!") would *still* let her lick his dick? I'm sure she'd toss back her sugar-rimmed gimlet, thrilled.

I'll bet Farrah, an actual Warhol muse, would race over in her two-door Mercedes to his too-expensive-for-his-age house and ring the bell. He'd open it, thinking it was the Indian food he'd just ordered, tossing in a bonus cheese naan for sauce sopping. And there she'd be, fiftyish hair slightly more brittle than the buoyant bouncy locks of the poster of his youth. But he didn't care. He'd *still* fuck her. She evokes in him his—and I'm kind of proud of this one—six-million-dollar manhood. I'm sure she'd totally appreciate his spastic lovemaking skills, confused and overwhelmed, as he hunched into her magnificent iconic blondness. He couldn't help but think about his Steve Austin doll with bionic grip and an actual telescopic eye as he spewed out a premature load, just imagining the silhouetted opening credits of *Charlie's Angels*. Blooooop, praying he can make it past the Kate Jackson as meter maid part.

If you have the opportunity to sleep with a Farrah type, go ahead. It's not like whatever I say is going to sway you. You *should* do it. Do it a bunch of times for good measure, if you can. But if you wind up marrying an actress, don't be surprised if you spend quite a bit of time allaying her insecurities and fears. Because the prettiest packages usually need the most reassurance. And when the most beautiful person in the room all of a sudden gets older and can't rely on her physical package any longer, guess who is in charge of reassuring her diminishing looks with increasing compliments? That's you. And by then, you'll be old and exhausted.

2. Don't date bisexuals. (Too complicated until your picker is sharper.)

Bisexuals, please don't be mad at me. I'm not one of those people who believe it's a phase on the road to gay. It's an amazing and incredible thing to be emotionally and sexually available to 100 percent of the population. However, for people whose partner-pickers don't function well, you're just too complicated. Dealing with bisexuals requires a higher skill level at first, so let's not make it hard on the people who choose poorly. It's like trying to ride a bucking bronco when you have no clue what a saddle is. It opens up way too many emotional tributaries for the common man to handle.

If you're a guy dating a bi-girl, you may think this is hot and sexy. But word to the wise: she likes to *fuck* other women. It's not just a sexy skit for your pleasure. And, chances are, if she's a girl lover, she also likes to emotionally connect with women. Which will *double* the amount of boring emotional talks you hate, but have to have. Trust me, the potential for experiencing a three-way won't cover the amount of time you'll waste on the "I'm-not-getting-my-emotional-needs-met" girl-blather. Which any girl who likes girls has naturally grown to expect. Fact: A straight female has spent a lifetime curbing her expectations of the amount of emotional processing a straight man can endure. A straight woman is your best-case scenario with that.

And here's a super-big piece of news: being bisexual doesn't actually mean she is *automatically* open to three-ways. Bisexual just means that particular person is open to loving and/or fucking both genders. So you may *never* get this elusive magical night that you're hoping to boast to your friends about. "My dick was in one vagina, then it was inside another. One mouth, then the other! Four tits! One cock!" You may have put in hours and hours of dialogue with your bi-girlfriend about her emotions that will *never, ever pay off. Ever.* You may be digging a well that will never yield water. You will die a thirsty man while still putting in all that goddamned sweaty, dusty digging effort. You will just have spent a lifetime in circuitous conversations, only imagining her going down on a woman. And if that's true, you may as well just imagine your straight girlfriend fingering a lady.

3. *Don't date someone way smarter than you. And don't date someone way dumber.*

This is one of those rules that is very tough to gauge at the beginning. You're so caught up in the fucking that whatever she says, you imbue her with a certain mental acumen. It is only when you take that person out of the bedroom and into real-life situations that her stupidity may register. If you're not totally sure how smart she may be, take her out to meet your friends and family—not that they will tell you the truth. They will lie to your face. No one will tell you your new girlfriend is too dumb. They will just wait for you to realize it.

This process takes a long time. How can you tell if your new woman just isn't keeping up? If you tell a story and she stares at you blankly, don't assume this means she's in a higher place of understanding. (See Jerzy Kosinski's *Being There.*) If you find yourself always asking, "Do you know what I mean? Do you get what I'm saying? Do you know what I'm talking about?" these are your own clues that you are dating the less smart. You: "No, you're not understanding my point. Are you being purposefully obtuse?" Her: a blank stare. You: "Do you know what obtuse means?" Her: "Of course. It's a triangle." Or, after taking your new girlfriend to a friend's wedding, Her: "That was amazing, they're such a cute couple. Are you ready to throw graffiti at the bride?" You, with teeth grinding: "Did . . . you mean . . . confetti?"

Conversely, the too-smart woman will make *you* feel dumb. If you are the one struggling to understand the anecdotes, the references—what is preindustrialized London? Anything about the Roman aqueducts or jet propulsion. You still think the native language of Sweden is candy. If you are constantly reminding yourself to google the meaning of the topics that she brings up, then she is too smart for you. Especially if you feel too embarrassed to ask, "What the hell are you talking about?"

You'll try to nod with seeming intuition, making your eyes sparkle with comprehension. It will take a while before you are found out. When she's talking about something you find tedious, or you don't understand, try to stop yourself from saying that aloud. You may even risk asking questions about her wide body of knowledge on things that interest you not at all. But be advised, you will reveal that you don't know shit.

4. Don't date the unemployed.

Some people don't care about money. They don't mind paying every time. It does something for their self-esteem, or it doesn't even occur to them to care. Good for them! Find them and date them. The downside of being the person who always pays is that it creates a legitimate power imbalance. Like boss/employee, it creates a not-so-sexy dynamic. Traditionally, we're more used to the guy paying, although you still shouldn't have to pay all the time. The rule isn't "Don't date those who are paid less than you" or "Don't date the people who love it when you pay." It's "Don't date the unemployed."

Having a job creates an identity, a self-confidence and equality. It creates balance between two people, even if their pay packet is extremely different. That equality can't be bought with the laying down of a credit card every time the bill comes. I'm not talking about if you get married; I'm talking about when you have the entire world's population to choose from. Don't date someone who can't get her shit together enough to pay for her own things, even if they're of a lesser quality than yours. You don't want to marry someone who has never purchased a couch, even if it's a crappy one.

If she is being supported by her parents, this dynamic creates a whole other dimension of unnecessary competitions, entitlement, and comparisons. If she simply can't figure out what it is she wants to be when she grows up enough to get any kind of job, that's another host of headaches. And if this woman can't get a job in whatever field she has chosen, she will feel doubly dumb, insecure, and inadequate. All of this creates a series of unnecessary frictions and fights. Which will stop you from fucking.

I'm just trying to clear the path for you to fuck. If I had to take out all the "Don'ts" and pare it down to one simple "Do," it would be "Date your equal." And that includes financial economics as well as emotional considerations. She doesn't need to make the same kind of money as you do, or even be in the same ballpark—but she should feel that she can survive and be on her own independent path, without your economic subsistence.

5. *Don't date someone much younger or older than you.* *(Seven years max in either direction, please.)*

I don't care about age, per se. Maybe you don't either. It's enough that you obey the statutory laws of the land. Maybe you're aroused by wrinkles; that's fine, too. But here is a cautionary tale about dating people beyond this seven-year span: you are always going to be in a different phase of life than she is.

I have a twenty-six-year-old friend; let's call him Jason. No, wait, he's young, so let's call him Jax. Jax, with his cute, off-white canvas tennis shoes and stripey shirts, started dating an eighteen-year-old. (This breaks the rule only slightly; just eight years younger instead of seven.) He thought this was super sexy at the time. I thought he was acting like a teenage fuck pig; barely legal, but shockingly, it worked! This couple, whom I wound up adoring, dated for five happy years.

Then all of a sudden, Jax was thirty-one. A legitimately normal age to want to get married and start a family. But his girlfriend was only twenty-three. And in practical years, because they started dating when she was so young, she'd never experienced anything but a world with Jax. She went directly from her parents' house to his house, so she was basically still eighteen inside. He was ready to buy her a ring and, even though she loved him and wanted to marry him in an abstract way, she knew she wasn't ready to accept it. She had other things to explore first. This is the best-case scenario for it not working out. It totally worked until it totally didn't. But this age gap was a cruel dagger in an otherwise great relationship. You can't trick time.

Another example to the extreme reverse. When I was in college, my friend Lauren, then a junior, started sneakily dating our salt-and-pepper-haired professor. Canyoubelieveit?! He was sexy and, however metaphorically, had suede elbow patches sewn onto his corduroy blazer. A real erudite know-it-all windbag, but he was so smart, he'd read every esoteric book in the library. (Remember libraries? Those dusty, old museums used to house dusty, old books? Now, they're where the homeless go to take shits.)

The professor was "worldly." Late at night, while reading James Tate's poetry, he'd pinch sardines with his fingers and eat them, dripping with oil straight from the tin, staining the volume's page corners. The professor had once been to Malta. He boasted the exotic age of forty-eight! We couldn't believe how lucky Lauren was to participate in this steamy, stomach-churning affair.

But wait—Lauren actually said yes when he proposed to her. Moments before her 250-guest wedding, while I was wearing an eggplant velvet scoop-necked bridesmaid dress, I did the unthinkable. I dragged her aside (and away from the sixty-two-year-old groomsman I'd been assigned to hobble down the aisle with—the old dude even had a cane) and begged her to reconsider marrying the professor. Not so much the man, but the life of being the wife of someone so much her senior. She wasn't even mad at me. Thanked me. Said she understood my panic. Had it herself. But, mind-bogglingly, she walked down that aisle.

Even more mind-boggling is that all these years later, she is still married to him. He is twenty-six years older than Lauren; a year younger than her own father. He recently had hip-replacement surgery, and is still lucky enough to boast a full head of cotton-colored hair to match his thicket of white pubes. This man—who has read the entire library, and turns up his snooty nose at you because you have not—doesn't own an iPad or a cell phone because "they're too hard to figure out." All waitresses, all of them, mistake Lauren for his daughter or caregiver. What was extremely sexy at twenty-two ("I pretended to lose my keys in his classroom. He was *very* happy to help me look for them . . .") is now just a wrinkled pile of rosaceous obligation, scotch-induced stomach bloat, and regret.

I reiterate: the dating age limit is seven years maximum, please. It's not that it's not sexy in the short term—it is! If you are just there to fuck the young or fuck the old, that's fine. Do it! Intergenerational hookups are awesome! "Tell me about how a pay phone worked!" "What do you mean you never learned cursive because you always had a keyboard?" But things can happen. Feelings can occur, and you can start the long process of rationalizing the unrationalizable. (See above re: the less smart; see below re: the drunks.) It's just that in the long term, in these two examples, the datee is either in a different place than you are emotionally or, in the case of the elderly, you are resentful. You're quietly, passively rooting for their death, so that your life may begin.

6. No drug addicts or nonrecovering alcoholics.

It is totally fine to date or marry sober, nonpracticing drug addicts and alcoholics. Good for them for going hard and then seeking recovery. Their clear-headedness and ability to self-examine may actually service your relationship if you can handle all the shopping, gambling, emotionally driven rants, overly hurt feelings, and food- and sex-addiction that drug and alcohol deprivation stimulates. But for all the users, the too-heavy drinkers and drug lovers out there, just accept this excess as a red flag and move the hell along.

People who are "experimenting" with drugs in their thirties are no longer experimenters. They are time-proven and tested *doers*. Consider this as well: if *you* are an alcoholic, you don't need someone else to party with you. Why would you want to take turns cleaning up someone else's vomit or tucking someone else in, or worrying who is less drunk and actually slightly more capable of driving—when you could have a dedicated person doing it for you? Drunk people, date those who don't drink, if you are able. They are a natural yin-yang to your disgusting excess. Don't worry; they have a piece in the dynamic, too. They can take care of you while simultaneously judging you, so that they may feel better about themselves without examining why they are with a broken-down glutton like you.

But if you are not an alcoholic, you don't want to spend your life marveling or complaining, gauging and feeling powerless about someone else's self-abusive intake.

So just don't bother. If you can't tell at the beginning of a relationship if she is or isn't a drunk or druggie, ask if her parent/s like to drink and anesthetize to excess. If she complains about her boozy parents or crazy childhood, just stop dating this person. This shit is hereditary. Just avoid it. Move on before it snaps back at you. These fights and negotiations of chemical dependence soak up a lot of time when you could otherwise be fucking.

Chapter 4

Relationships
Wanting the Woman You've Got

"I'm staying in, guys. I'm finally getting the hang of how to intuit Zoe's needs."

The only thing you can trust about a woman is just when you think you've got her all figured out, boom! That's when she'll switch it up, wanting the exact opposite. You couldn't have predicted it. You can't ever stop learning; you may not relax behind a previous body of wisdom.

But, if you want to fuck the woman you are in a relationship with, here are the four key words that will consistently help you do it. Simply ask, "How was your day?" You may also add her personal name or "honey" or "baby" to the end of that interrogatory statement, if you wish. A comment that *you* may hear as complimentary, such as "Hey, have you lost weight?," will only start a fight. She will hear, "Up until this very second, you thought I was fat!" I get it. This is why you don't say much. You're never sure what will set her off. How can you know these words (that you think are kind) are really the kindling to your entire night's plan?

Goodbye SportsCenter, hello big fight culminating with going-to-get-her-toilet-paper-mostly-to-get-away-from-

her-but-also-to-help-her-blow-her-nose-and-wipe-away-her-tears-because-why-does-she-have-to-be-the-only
-one-to-think-of-buying-goddamn-Kleenex-around-here?
And, okay, maybe you're not a SportsCenter guy, but stop being so fucking literal, which is why she's always mad at you. *I'm* mad at you right now just for suspecting you might say this. Look, you had a plan for your night. And now it's gone, and you have to just pathetically look online for the score of the game because you missed it—because of the fight you could've easily avoided with the very simple "How was your day, baby?" That one tiny question is the key to watching live sporting events. (Or *whatever*, literal asshole!)

Always Ask for Her Advice

Another excellent fuck-helper is the little-used "Hey. I have this thing going on with _____ (my work, my boss, my hemorrhoid, my dad, your dad, the national debt—who cares; fill in the blank but eventually get to the following words) and *I could really use your advice on it.*"

Bonus: you may even find her opinion insightful and helpful, because she's used to analyzing every single nuance of every situation. Glean choice bits from what she says, and apply this concept to your problem. Without even realizing it, a piece of her advice may stick to you like an unshakeable piece of linguini at the bottom of the colander. Her opinion may actually register and remedy something, somewhere.

But that would only be a bonus; it's not why you're asking. *By asking what she feels* about any given matter, you are telling her that her opinion matters; that *she* matters. What she says is important to you. It also may convey to her that you realize you don't have all the goddamn answers about every single thing. You are not the know-it-all-dick-head you appear to be.

It's the old men-don't-want-to-ask-for-directions-disease (an epidemic that has mostly been ameliorated in modern times with the invention of MapQuest. Progress! Millions of lost hours saved!). The very *act of asking* her allows that you don't own all the solutions, but more importantly, *that her opinion is valued and sought after.* This powerful one-two punch will make her feel open to you emotionally and then, almost as if it were her idea, she may also be open to your dick.

This shit is subtle, too. Sometimes it can be gradual, so practice patience. She may have an accrued resentment; a thick emotional buildup from you *not* inquiring and *not* making these types of gestures for forever. So don't despair if the first couple of times you use these tools, they fall flat and the vaginal gate doesn't immediately open. It is most assuredly rusty. But, if you continue on this quest, asking and giving small considerations, she will invariably thaw. Practice these tips because not only will your life get way more livable via her happier attitude, but it will also include more sex—which in turn makes *you* way more livable. Ah, there's that cute little infinity symbol: "∞."

See, the thing is that men can sound tough and smell rough, but your egos are as fragile and sensitive as your testicles. The thing I recall about balls, is that they're soft and easily hurt. Your nuts are as sensitive as our girl-feelings. Men need to feel connected through sexual intimacy in order to be emotionally intimate. And women—well, we need to feel emotionally close in order to fuck. So you straight people have a constant dilemma. Everyone is in pursuit of something, but no one really gets his or her needs met unless one of you makes an active compromise. So one of you must start somewhere, or neither of you will ever get anywhere. This solution is the emotional equivalent of an app like Waze.

With the same awe and interest you gave a vagina the first time you met one, you should wonder how to deal with the woman attached to it every single day that you're in a relationship with her. I know this may seem excessive, but if you start taking it for granted, your attitude will backfire and start affecting the things you treasure most. I know you love her, but you also love what her happiness and contentment brings to you: consistent and pleasant access to the removal of semen from your balls. So making small allowances for her emotional needs will grant you a general pass of argument-free living and reliable vaginal admission.

You must put gas in your car. Sometimes you even wash the windshield or change the oil. You must do the equivalent of these things with your woman, or she will stop running. For the most effective and easy life, you must pay attention to her before the equivalent of her red dash-board lights go on. I'm not trying to be reductive of women, but we are built differently than you are. You want us not to notice you; you want to be left to your thoughts. But we want you to be sensitive to ours.

I Just Texted to Say I ♥ You . . .

You may get caught up in the everydayness of life and start taking this stuff for granted. Here's a tip. Approach your woman as if you're a scientist trying to ascertain something new. As if you've discovered an extraterrestrial in your bed. Study her discreetly so as not to make her aware that you're studying her at all. What does she eat? What does she drink? What temperature water does she prefer to clean herself with? Maybe she enjoys a certain kind of creamy emollient to protect her alien skin. What kind of sleep habits does she have? How does she take care of her young? Does she make pleasant murmury sounds if you offer your services of helping her to rear her offspring?

Do not grow complacent. Be the iconoclast scientist that I know you can be. The stakes are huge. You must ask yourself, "How do I make her happy, so she doesn't take over the (my) world?" Or even less cataclysmic: "How can we peaceably coexist on Earth?" Be aware of her needs, and see what secrets of the galaxy this consideration can unlock. You are good at different things; perhaps you can be of service to one another and live in harmonious accord. You should approach the entire population of women with this same level of awe and wonder. Because women are that different from you. She is studying you and your needs just as carefully, even though you don't know it because she's better at it than you. Update: she's been doing it the whole time you've known her. You are only just learning about this now.

You think that in order to keep peace/have sex, you need to do little things like bring her flowers. Flowers are great, but you're essentially giving us something else to throw away in five days. You will never notice the dead flowers or smelly, viscous, mildewy flower water that stinks up the whole apartment. So now we have to dump the rotten flowers, take out garbage, and decide whether or not to hold on to and wash the not-so-cute vase they came in. Essentially, you are giving us three annoying chores.

If you're just trying for adorable, one flower is kind of cute. Again, it's "not the size of the bouquet, it's what you do with it." Also, if you go overboard, it's like throwing away a few hundred-dollar bills. If you're going to do this, I would personally prefer to own something more permanent (clothes, jewels, new technological equipment) or even an interactive experience that says you're thinking about me. A picnic you pick out at the grocery store after you tell me that you're going to handle dinner. Now you've done two nice things, instead of blowing a bunch of money on tomorrow's floral garbage.

Whenever the phone rings and it's you, know that she's already suspicious. It's (most likely) you calling to say you can't complete something you've assured her you'll do.

Can't make it home for dinner. Can't be there to watch your son play "Three Blind Mice" with a plastic recorder at his Pumpkin Harvest recital. You are calling to report a deficiency of some kind. She's learned to associate your name popping up on her phone as negative. You're Pavlov's dog that diarrheas all over her most expensive white rug. Sorry, but this is your fault. She's scared to answer your calls because disappointing her is pretty much the only time you ever call her.

But life isn't over yet. You've created this feeling, and you can just as easily change it. Call her just to say you miss her. This will blow her ass away. "Hey . . . I was just thinking about you and wanted to call." "And . . .?" she will suspiciously wonder. She will undoubtedly suspect you of fucking her tittsiest friend, Gabby, who you totally "don't get why everyone thinks is so hot." (You do. Gabby's totally hot; she's got those massive tits.) But no, you're just calling because you miss her. If you don't have time for a conversation *or are sensitive to the fact that she may not*, just text "I miss you." Or the even less effortful "Miss you." I've even programmed custom typing shortcuts, "mu" and "ly," into my phone to turn these simple letters into complex, life-sustaining emotions. For the limbless who still love to fuck, poke a heart-shaped emoticon into your phone with your nose.

The First Fight Is the Microcosm of All Future Fights

I have, thus far, avoided talking with any specificity about my own relationship experiences, because the ones I had before kids had such little stakes, and the one I had with kids meant too much in real life to discuss in any satisfying detail. I mean, no matter what, the person I had children with will always be my babies' mama. But I can share what I learned from that relationship (which was way more about procreation than it ever was about fucking; should've been my first giant clue it wouldn't work out). But the most amazing things came out of that relationship: my beautiful, genius son and my gorgeous, hilarious daughter. But my old relationship's failure can serve you. Let me pay for your therapy with my own. Here's the headline I gleaned from all of it:

WHATEVER THE TOPIC OF YOUR FIRST FIGHT WILL INVARIABLY BE THE TOPIC OF YOUR LAST FIGHT.

With my baby-mama, our first fight was "the kettle fight." It happened in, like, month one or two. Who can remember—it's stacked underneath so many bigger, huger, louder, crazier, cry-zier battles. Men, you may want to skip over this next part; the following fight between two lesbians doesn't involve Catholic schoolgirl uniforms or titty pinching. No, this fight is frighteningly dry. It's even worse than the very worst of any of your most banal straight-people fights. It may be the least sexy conflict in the history of conflict—frankly, par for that relationship's course. But it is the trembler, the rumbling of the earth years ahead of the Big One. If only we all knew to pay attention to our own first fights, we'd either know how this shit was going to end or, even better, be ahead of it enough to work on the relationship.

Okay. So. Let me set the super-unsexy stage. I was hungry. I wanted instant oatmeal. Couldn't find a kettle. So, I went out and bought a utilitarian kettle. It was metal with a black circley thing that set off a helpful reminder whistle when the water boiled. I heated water until it was hot. Poured and stirred. Ta-da, delicious oatmeal! I set my nice, new kettle down on the stovetop.

My as-flavorful-as-oatmeal ex—let's call her Sarah— came in and was startled by the aesthetic choice I'd made regarding the kettle. "It's ugly," she said. "I don't like it." Me: "It's a kettle." "Cheap," she added. Hey, I chose it. I paid for it. In my opinion, it was neither, but I said, "It served its function; it heated water. Now, my belly is full of satisfying oats." She said, "Oh no, no, no, how could you buy this without my input?" Me: stupefied, truly not comprehending, "Huh . . . ?" She insisted I should've consulted her. "This kettle sits *atop* the stove," she contemptuously explained, as if I should also feel the stinging emotional slap still resonating on her cheek. "It's a visual choice, so I should've been included in this matter."

I truly didn't get it. You probably don't either. "Aren't I allowed to go out and buy something with my own money that meets my needs without consulting you?" "No." Which someone else might deliver as "No!" but the absence of her exclamation point still poked me as if she'd used one. She was adamant: "Not if it affects the household aesthetics." (I so wish this story was juicier, but this is about as exciting as it ever got, God bless.)

So what happened over the next ten years was that I began to defer my design feelings, and subsequently my *feeling*-feelings, because it always created too much conflict if they didn't meld perfectly with her many opinions. She, who hated personal conflict more than actual war, most assuredly did the same. Big tips are coming now, the most important ever: When you both stop honestly communicating, your relationship is over. When people stop connecting, allowing for individuality, risking, sharing, trying, opening, being willing to listen, reflect, change, compromise, grow, give the thing it hurts the most to give . . . well, you get it.

The first fight is the microcosm of all future fights. It's the flavor of what the rest of the fights taste like, no matter what. They can all be boiled down to this nugget; this essence of the first fight. So please pay attention to it. Because whatever that dynamic is, it will be the same fight you fight about year after year, in whatever form, until you either accept this in the DNA of each other, or the relationship dies. That's a fact. With me and my ex, I guess it was tough to look at a kettle fight and think that was going to be the toxin that would ultimately poison our water. Seemed pretty small at the time. But pay exceptional attention to the small stuff, too, please.

You Can Only Change Yourself

People say that love is blind. (Please don't confuse blind love with what I talked about earlier, the "Vagina Effect" or

"Cock Hypnosis.") Love's being blind is a much more advanced form of this disease. It's after the initial drug of fucking wears off, and you actually love this person, then, the escalation, the progression, is failing to see their flaws. You look through a dirty, distorted lens. You can't see the truth clearly. How they are and who they are and how they behave in the world is skewed by your love. Your love overrides everything, which is nice, in a myopic sort of way.

But if you think about a relationship as a really, really long, destinationless road trip where stops are made and cheesy crackers are mashed into the cracks of the seats and tiny passengers get on and get off and engines seize and tires blow, what you need throughout the many-mile journey is the purity of sight. Look at the road, listen to each other's opinions, steer the vehicle, hold hands, use Wet-Naps, get the car washed even though it'll just get dirty again, give each other breaks distracting the kids, take turns driving and being in charge of the music, give everyone a chance to pick which drive-thru, make sure we stop when someone needs to pee, even if you don't have to. Respect each other; even if you disagree about the route, you're still in this car together.

During this long, exhausting, endless road trip, we must see each other and the reality of the road. Because if love is blind, this car will fucking crash. We must look at each other for who we really are, and—here's the most difficult thing in the whole goddamn world, as well as the biggest reality—*accept your partner as they are.* Huge true fact: you cannot change anyone. You can only change yourself.

(And you can barely change you, and you're inside your-self!) Isn't that the worst? Wouldn't it be so much easier if we could change our partner to suit our own desires and needs? If this were possible, Sarah might've returned my kettle, bought her version (the more costly, aesthetic to *her* eye pleasing), and then maybe I would've been allowed to make oatmeal.

Okay, well, I was just eating because I was hungry. I was so very, very hungry throughout that relationship because of a hundred thousand shades of the kettle fight. I will be very honest now. Time to admit it. Many—maybe even most—of the fights I provoked because I was hungry. I was hungry, and I stopped feeding myself with little things like buying kettles to make oatmeal. I stopped taking care of my own needs because they created too much conflict. I am the one who stopped buying kettles. That's my fault. See why I don't use myself as an example? So unglamorous, this kettle fight. But the message is an extremely important one.

A Relationship Primer

To snazz things up after that cautionary oatmeal tale, here are a few quick relationship primer tricks.

Show interest in her life, and the stuff she talks about. Ask about her work or annoying events she has planned, dinners out with her friends, her visit to the ophthalmolo-gist, her cousin's surgery, etc. Write these boring events down when she initially talks about them, and later, remem-ber to ask her about these things. Make her think you give a shit. Be an actor. "Hey, did your aunt ever narrow down what brand of white noise machine to buy?" It will make her feel like she matters. When she feels like she matters, she will trust you. When she trusts you, she will want to fuck you. Think of the opening of her legs as if it were an old-fashioned castle drawbridge: "Lower the bridge!" That heavy rusted gate was only opened for those whom they trusted.

When she looks like she's in her head about something while she's unloading the dishwasher, even though you're sure you're guilty of absolutely zero, ask her gently, "What are you thinking about, baby?" Whatever the thing she is obsessing about (e.g., that you never ever empty the fucking dishwasher) will disappear because you noticed she was distracted. She will say nothing about it, but she'll feel lighter because you asked. If you can handle the advanced version of this, just simply take over whatever chore she is doing. Tell her, "Oh, honey, let me do that." (A healing, helpful action!) "You're always doing that." (I see you.) "They're just as much my dishes." (I appreciate all you do, thank you!) "Why don't you just *tell me about your day*?" "What happened with *fill-in-the-blank*?" Your *(specific you've texted yourself, so that you might recall)* coworker's rental car issue?" (You are interested in the details.)

She will fuck you for this. She may even blow you. A hand-job at least. Because she feels seen, heard, and taken care of; even empathized with. You even ostensibly remembered the mind-numbingly dull story about her annoying coworker's abscessed foot. I know this sounds so dumb, and you're thinking, "What's her problem? I'm not a mind reader. Why doesn't she just *ask* me to empty the dishwasher?" Here's why: She doesn't want to have to ask you. She wants you to think of it yourself, and then do it.

Don't Make Her Be Your Mommy

Now, that's doing two things, I know. But if she has to ask, that puts her in the bossy or naggy or mommy position, and all she wants you to do is see it for yourself. See her, know her, intuit her needs. You both need the dishwasher emptied, but she usually does it. Stop patting yourself on the back for semirinsing a plate you used and sticking it in the machine. Do you think the clean dishes leap out of the machine and put themselves back up into the cupboard? No. *She* does it! It's her! I know it all sounds simple and/or small, but if you're more attentive to the tiny things it never dawned on you to consider before, this will add up to way more fucking for you.

Don't mistake being a good dad with being a good partner; aka, don't confuse parenting with partnering. It's great if you're spending your Sunday at your daughter's soccer match. Kudos for doing the minimum. Clap yourself on the back if you're giving your dirty-assed kids a bath or dropping them at the mall, or taking that absent-minded son of yours to cobble together a last-minute frontier costume he needs by tomorrow morning for school. That's all great and amazing, but listen up—you made these kids, too. It's not just her job to do all this mind-numbing shit.

No one person can do it well, especially if she has a job, too, which almost 70 percent of moms do today. So, as much as she may appreciate your doing your part, please don't confuse that with giving to her as a partner.

Maybe she doesn't have the expectation that you *will* do this stuff. But you *should* be doing it. You don't have to *want* to do it; she doesn't want to do it, either. But, somehow, all this child care and home maintenance gets done— who do you imagine is getting the job done? Now, if you *don't* do it and she doesn't seem to expect it or notice or care, then congratulations! You're currently in possession of an awesome, albeit ignorant woman. So if you're skating by in life, unnoticed, and she's running around without resentment, for God's sake at least be grateful about it.

Scribble her a note of love and appreciation, using your human hand and ink and real paper from trees. Say thank you. Go down on her (see chapter 8). Tickle her back a little at night for all the extra, amazing things you take for granted—so that you can sit on your fat ass feeling resentful that you don't get to fuck that raspy-voiced new woman at work who would never ever fuck you, even if you weren't married or had a head of hair or a decent personality.

Because if you have little kids, I'm going to tell you something about your wife that you do not want to know: *she hasn't had a bowel movement with the bathroom door closed since your children were born.* "Mommy's in the potty, honey! Here! In here! Having privacy! *Privacy!* Oh, no, it's okay. You can be in here, too. Yes, Mommy has to wipe her own bottom, just like she wipes yours. Yes. Oh. Right. That's true. That *is* Mommy's poo-poo."

Don't even start about tampons. *You* try explaining what the hell one of those things is and does to a neck-craning curious three-year-old. All this is to say that if you're debating whether or not to offer to pick up dinner on the way home or fix the gate or make the bed or tell her that she looks pretty, even if it's a total fucking lie, just do it all. For God sakes, maybe even just look her in the eye a moment too long and when she accuses you of acting weird, tell her you're grateful for all the shit she does.

That the little stuff adds up to big stuff. Tell her that you notice, that you appreciate, that your life couldn't feel the beautiful way it does without her, and all the things she's sure you don't notice. Say you're blown away by all she does. Again, aside from all this being true, you will get sex. Oh. If she is a lazy, depressed, pill-popping, binge eater who yells about everything and always appears to have what looks like potato chip grease on her forehead and can't be bothered with you or your kids, say none of this.

Maybe you do a lot with your kids, for her, and even around the house. Maybe you're amazing and acknowledge everything she does that's amazing, too. Great job! Okay, but still. Just because you're sanding a door or changing a lightbulb doesn't mean you are intimately connecting with her. Even though you perceive doing these things *for* her, don't mistake the time you take painting the bathroom doorjamb or cleaning the gutters for connecting with her. Taking out the trash doesn't equal saying "I love you."

I know, I know, it totally *seems* like it should. Why else would you be doing that stuff? The list to keep a relationship afloat appears to be endless and time consuming and taxing. You may ask, "How am I supposed to remember all this stuff?" Well, know this: if you don't, she will. It will accrue in the form of resentment. It's not her job to desire to spend time with you alone *and* to get a babysitter *and* to make a goddamned restaurant reservation or purchase movie tickets in advance. You can do all these things, too. And if you do, the resentment accrual will be slightly washed away. And you will get sex.

Be on Her Team

Oh, here's a very quick and easy one. Be on her team. When listening to her nightly stories of how she was sidestepped for whatever promotion, or when she's nattering shit about the other parents at your daughter's school, or about buying homeopathic flea medicine for the cat you despise, just be on her side. Agree with her. It is not your responsibility to represent her perceived opponents' viewpoint. Don't "see it from the other side, another perspective." She won't care. She will resent you. You have just become another adversary in her life. Keep your real reaction to yourself. Bite the tongue of your nature to lecture and edify. The key to making all this talk go away is a simple three-part procedure:

1. Just listen, don't advise. "If I were you . . ." (you're *not* her).

2. With matters that concern only her, no matter how you feel, just agree with her position. It's not your problem; it's hers, and so her feelings are the only ones that really matter.
3. Empathize with her. Use key interactive/empathetic phrases such as "Oh God, what did you say to that?" "I can't believe she/he did/said that." "I'm so sorry, honey." "How do you feel?" "I get why you feel that way." "That's a really hard position to be in."

One. Two. Three. Now, you get hard and get in position.

There Are No Trophies for Being Right

Let go of needing to be right. This is maybe the hardest thing of all for men to learn. *It does not matter if you're right.* I will say it again, because it is a very advanced concept to wrap your head around: Who cares if you're right? No one is keeping an imaginary ledger of your sliverlike wins over the course of a lifetime. There are no trophies in marriage for who wins more fights. Because here is the truth: you will never win, even if she seemingly capitulates to your point. The argument will bleed energy, emotional and otherwise, from your life when you are in pursuit of comfort and sleep and food and quiet and cheese and TV and fucking and the glorious, ephemeral feeling right after fucking: having fucked.

If these are your basic goals, why do you need to be right? Be right at work or with your friends—who neither feed your kids, nor suck your dick. No one is keeping score of your rightness. You don't get a Kobe-like three-pointer at the buzzer and a cheering crowd ovation for your wife acknowledging your irrelevant argument wins.

"When will it end? When will the fight/argument/disagreement/processing around it be over? When can I get back to myself and my underpants and my iPad and my own personal thoughts? When will she shut the fuck up? She's made her point, like, twenty-seven times! When is enough, enough?"

This is a hard one to answer; not because the answer is so difficult, but because it's so easy that it will haunt your entire history of time-wasting fights. After you hear my solution, you're going to feel completely dumb because the answer was there all along. In *The Wizard of Oz*, it's Dorothy looking down at her magical ruby red slippers after Glinda the Good Witch says, "You had the power all along." For you, the clicking of the ruby slippers will get you out of your fight and back home to Kansas, post-tornado. You will now get to eat Auntie Em's homemade fried chicken; yum.

Here's all you have to do—and it sounds way harder than it actually is. Let go of the feelings around it, and simply say the words out loud. Say them fully formed and generously: "I'm sorry." See, the thing is, in order for her to move past this fight, you need to acknowledge her point. For her to know that you've actually heard her, and marked her rightness in your brain, you need to say this aloud as if it's a verbal stamp. You need to make an auditory notation of her victory. Just say it if you want the nonsense to stop. Especially say it because she's probably right in some way.

But who cares if she's wrong? So what if you believe you're totally right? I'm telling you, if you crave your post-fight underpants moment, if you want this verbal sparring to stop, what the hell does it cost you, really? Don't you gain more than you lose? Just say it with conviction: "You're right. I see your point, (*use name here*). I'm sorry." If you want extra credit, toss in something like "I'm going to try and be more aware of that." Or "I'm going to try to work on that." Whatever this word combo, it will act like a vaccine for all temporary annoyances. It will debrittle her. It will catch her off-guard. And then you'll be a little surprised when the fight is over and she says aloud some version of "Thank you. I appreciate you saying so." And then she will either leave you to your underpants moment or, even better, because she has just been validated for her emotions, she will fuck you—which is much better than an unresolved smoldering argument.

Don't Give Your Opinion Unless You're Asked

Another scoop of advice is self-censor any negative comments about our looks. I know you think you're helping by giving your opinion—the one we never asked for. But big or small, thin or thick, we women have obsessed about our bodies for our whole lives, so that when you say something

even vaguely negative, we retain it. We carry it with us forever, like being burned with acid. We retain anything that
criticizes us; anything that calls us out.

An example: when I was in fifth grade, I briefly danced
in a class. Not the required do-si-do of the mandatory
square dance, but a real shimmy-shimmy-shake. I let go
amongst my eleven-year-old peers, felt the heart of the
music, and cut loose with a brimming smile. Some girl,
Carrie Shaughnessy, who got her period way before everyone else and thus had the tits to prove it, said aloud to a
small group of impressionable girls that I "couldn't dance."
I had "no rhythm." She laughed and pointed. I saw them
gang-laughing in hilarious agreement, a villainous slo-mo.

The truth: I have literally never danced again. Anywhere. For any reason. Preferring instead to make fun of
others as they show the most vulnerable sides of themselves. I'm sorry if I've ever hurt anyone's feelings with these
word-bullets. I'm jealous of your freedom, your lack of
self-possession, your willingness to look like an asshole
and be open to the Carrie Shaughnessys of the world.

Girls invariably become the women who retain all
negative remarks, while anything positive flies up and out
the window. Women's fragile psyches are like naked sticks
of butter, revealing every CSI-like fingerprint of everyone
who ever brushed up against them too hard. So no matter
how tiny the compliment, focus on the positive side of
things because she will retain any negative morsel forever.
And she does have total recall of all of it. She is the Dewey
Decimal System of the cataloguing of emotional slights.

She can conjure up the most obscure, innocuous remark you made six years ago to prove her point today. How does she retain that, you wonder? Because it hurt her feelings. Avoid hurting these if you'd prefer more fucking.

Also, the thing that repels you about a woman is the very thing, once you're in love with her, that you kind of adore. It's the special thing you treasure. The lumpy butt, the sandbag thighs; it's the secret that you can't discuss with your friends. But you appreciate your woman's weakness, because it becomes a part of your territory. And you're territorial because you're a guy. Yes, you'd make fun of someone else's lady with that same issue, but that shit's not yours, so who cares?

Conversely, the things that drew you to your woman to begin with—that adorable way she eats, how she loves to stay up late, how she wants to show you all her loser boyfriends from her junior high school yearbook; all those things that made you fall in love with her in the first place—are the things that will cause you to clench your teeth, bellow with rage, complain inside your head. Everything you initially loved about her will shift with time-worn familiarity and turn into the grit in your spinach.

Why Men Cheat

A relationship is serious, tedious business. You are agreeing to fuck the same pussy forever. Squeeze only these tits. Kiss only this mouth. What a dire and dangerous contract. But even more than the sexual, you're agreeing to talk to her *before* and *after* sex *for forever*. Till you drop dead. That's what the contract says: "'til death." What an unsexy deal when laid out like that. People spend so much time working out fiscal realities in marriage, stuff like prenups, but no one's talking about having to fuck this same individual forever. Where's the fine print in the contract about that? You can change houses, make new children, watch all your parents die . . . but place penis in singular vagina—that's the nonnegotiable. Ludicrous when you spell it out, right? Your penis just got a life sentence in prison. Your penis and her vagina are in lockup.

Not too long ago, I was listening to a newly engaged Adam Levine on *Howard Stern* while he was addressing this concept. I wondered what we're all wondering here with this guy. Say it with me: "Why would Adam Levine ever get married?" Even to a professionally pretty person like Behati Prinsloo, a Namibian supermodel (I wish this were my description). And who knows, maybe she's a super-*nice*-model, too. But won't she—someday anyway—get old and tedious, too? Won't someday all those vowels in her name start to sag and droop? And even if she remains as gorgeous and kind and juicily lettered as she was on the day they got married, she still possesses only the one original vagina.

Why, when you are a handsome and rich, relevant rock star, with such a terrifically square jaw, a bar mitzvah under your belt and a great five o'clock shadow, would you confine your choice to just the one? When asked this question by Stern, Adam very astutely admitted, "I don't think as a man you ever stop being attracted to women, and it's a turbo-fucked-up situation for me. Is it worth sacrificing? You make a commitment. You choose." That's a huge choice. I mean, if Adam Levine can choose, how the hell can you even consider cheating on your woman? Can you imagine the level of top-shelf ass he has to rebuff?

Now, as we know, most of these high-profile celebrity marriages (congratulations, Kevin Bacon/Kyra Sedgwick!) don't wind up being very successful. And, beyond the *de rigeur* with-a-name-like-Levine circumcision, we really don't know the truth about what the hell goes on inside Adam Levine's underpants. But when you're famous, there are only two ways you can guarantee that the women you cheat with don't tell people that you're secretly fucking. Either she disappears under mysterious circumstances forever, or she keeps quiet because she has just as much to lose as you do. Meaning that, when you're famous, you should cheat with an equally famous person.

But how does a normal person last a lifetime without sacrificing his or her marital vows? Some sobering statistics: 57 percent of men and 54 percent of women admit to cheating on their spouse. That's a huge amount of people fucking around on each other after a bunch of oral and written contracts swearing they won't do so. So, why do people cheat? Answer: Because other people have different cocks and pussies than their husbands and wives, and don't come with the same endless amount of emotional upkeep.

Do people cheat because they are sick of the same stories, positions, and private parts? Well, yes, probably. My own suspicion of why they cheat is because we are, ultimately, weird animals. We lose all sense of right and wrong in the moments when we are charged up with flirtation or the dangerous adrenaline associated with flirting. Once you get past a certain point, like the aforementioned boiling kettle, it's pretty difficult not to do. Tip: try not to get to that point.

The 80/20 Rule in Relationships

Based on the Italian economist Vilfredo Pareto's principle, the 80/20 rule has also been applied to relationships. The rule says that in any given decent relationship, you're going to receive about 80 percent of what you need from your partner. And then, because we are greedy pigs driven by animal urges and desires, when we meet someone outside our relationship, even though they may only provide the 20 percent of what we need (the exact percentage we are lacking in our primary relationship), we trade it all away for that little piece that we are missing. After things settle down a bit, we might realize that what we have left is only that 20 percent. We don't realize how good we had it. By only focusing on the negative, we fucked it all up and lost a solid B for a big, fat F.

So why do men, in particular, cheat? There are tons of excuses: "She criticizes and nags me." "She doesn't look like the woman I married. Those three kids wrecked her body." "Hey, *she* stopped fucking *me*." "Men aren't built for monogamy." "It's just sex; it's not like I love her." Maybe the really real truth is probably very similar to what George

Mallory said of climbing Mount Everest: "Because it's there."

Men have the opportunity to do it more than they want *not* to do it. There are just so many vaginas out there in the world that go unfucked every day by faithful, married men. And, even if they are cheating, there are still so many new and extra holes walking around all the time, everywhere, unfilled by the penis in his pants. Men in long-term relationships are referring to new vaginas when they indicate wanting to go out to "get some strange." The unfamiliar one versus their own, too-familiar one. But then there's something else entirely: compartmentalization. Men lock it down, whereas women spill it out to dissect and process. Men love to keep a secret piece of self and soul. Something that is private and unhusked. They have a physiological need for internal privacy in a way that most women do not.

The Definition of Adultery

One guy I worked with, let's call him the Masturbator, spoke of the tiny office he built for himself out of drywall in his home's garage. The other writers in the room all referred to this place as "The Masturbatorium." He was very good at satisfying himself and was extremely prolific. He had, and probably still has, a pathological addiction to online pornography. So when I asked him, thinking it was rhetorical, if his wife of ten years knew how often he was in the office garage jerking off to barely legal Norwegian amputees, he was no less than incredulous: "What?! Of course not!"

Huh? I was genuinely stunned. This masturbation stuff was such a key fact about this man's personality. It's just how one would describe him. His hair was baby blond like Rolf Von Trapp's. He had a better-than-fine knowledge of power tools for someone whose trade was wordplay. And he was a YouPorn jack-off artist and citer of all things odd, disturbing, and sexually fetishistic contained within a computer. He was the guy who started the day with, "Hey, did you guys see . . . ?" Our answer was always collectively, "No."

With total authority, the Masturbator could teach a class on where to find the most interesting kink to self-stimulate to; some repellent, some intriguing, always informative. But his whack status was such a remarkable feature about him; it was the best way to describe this guy, and his own wife didn't know this? (None of the men in the room wondered about this, while I was completely blown away.) Maybe his wife knew everything about him except his illicit self-pleasuring; maybe it only ended up amounting to a tiny shred of his interior soul. But his exceptional jacking off prowess was the thing he kept private. Except to a roomful of professional colleagues whose ability to overshare personal details of their lives provided an instant closeness and false sense of intimacy. Oh, and not just *this* comedy room. Since TV writing is a nomadic culture, *many* rooms knew this fact about this guy.

Was this adultery? Well. That definition is up to you, and whomever you enter into a marriage contract with. But the amount of time he dedicated to making love to himself certainly ate into his theoretical time with his wife and two kids, so the volume of secrecy adds up to something on the scale of infidelity. I've met so many guys in so many of these rooms. His name could've been "the guy who loves to take his kids mini-golfing," "the one who tells dark stories about his violent, booze-saturated dad," "the guy who knows every esoteric 1970s male tennis player," or "the guy who cites the differences between Wednesday and Friday happy hour hors d'oeuvres at a strip club on La Brea." Or "the guy who *didn't realize until it was too late* that the prostitute who blew him in the back of his cousin's Lincoln might've had an Adam's apple." I mean, we all knew tons of private things about each other. But the Masturbator's wife didn't even know his nickname.

We'd go around about the definition of cheating. It differed between the genders, differed amongst gay people. What *is* cheating? It basically breaks down like this: women believe that if you exchange unfaithful energy, it's cheating. Men don't know what the fuck we're talking about. Guys are with Bill Clinton on this one; if you only come on her polycotton dress, you did not have sexual relations with that woman.

I'll say something fairly obvious: if you cheat in your relationship, it's pretty impossible to go back to the honesty and innocence of pre-cheating. Even if you never tell anyone, *you* know. Something major has occurred that leads you down a separate existence than your spouse. When you start out—unless you cheat on your honeymoon—the ingredient you have as a couple is truth. If truth changes for only one of you, then there is no more clarity. Your (quite differently wired) minds now see things from two separate vantage points, because one of you is missing big chunks of action. Some men have a "deny till you die" attitude that serves them well. Some men are so compartmentalized they actually believe their own versions of reality.

But just because they believe it, doesn't make it reality. After all, *they* must know. It must affect everything, at least subconsciously. Wouldn't all of life be tempered by particles of the secret? Like, aren't you thinking of it, mid–tooth brush, mid–cereal pour, mid–tucking in of your kids, mid–fucking your wife, and want to blurt, "Oh, I fucked a different hole." Doesn't it put a different hue on it all? Like dropping a solitary anchovy into cake batter, doesn't it make the entire cake taste like anchovies? And there's no taking it back. That fishy taste will be in every bite forever.

There are two ways to go, in terms of infidelity. Either be willing to compartmentalize every single thing you do after that—tuck it in, lock it down, be willing never to mention it, even to yourself—or, just don't do it to begin with.

I knew a woman who comported multiple clandestine relationships within her marriage for years and years, while her husband and kids obliviously lived with what they perceived as all she was capable of giving, emotionally and physically. They had no clue as to her secret, rich personal life. For the purpose of this story, let's call her "Mom." But you have to be the captain of Team Narcissism or part serial killer to do this successfully. It sort of shortchanges everyone's experience, right? She assumed her husband (let's call him "Dad") didn't have a right to know the truth about his own wife, or life. She assumed that her own truth was more important than everyone else's.

Facts all fell out when she was "ready to be honest," which gobbled up years of everyone's perceived reality. And for their kids, it wound up creating a life they *thought they had*, but one that turned out not to be very real. In hindsight, what was true? What wasn't ribboned with lies? Well, I have definitely figured out this part: even if kids don't *overtly* know that one of their parents is cheating at the time, it models something absent for them; a disconnection.

If you cheat. It's a cycle. You fuck, and it's incredible. You confuse this fuck tonic for love. It's so lava coated and toxic and sexy and crazy. But you are detonating everything you know. You hurt people. You hurt you. All in the name of the feeling of *love*. You stay with the new person because it feels like it's true love. It's amazing, I mean look how she made you feel . . . then as time passes, time heals. Your ex moves on. She's happy, kids seem good. Better than ever. And then there you are, feeling the same as you used to, but lying next to someone new, wondering what the common denominator is in all of your relationships that make you so miserable. Hey, stupid! It's *you*.

Tips and Tricks

I know you hate it when she's needy. But she's needy because she has needs. Some of these are bottomless pits that you had nothing to do with digging. Her daddy dug them or her mommy, or her lack-of or too-much of either or both of them. All you can do is not be reactive to them. Don't trip in the hole. Take them at face value. If you can help her, do it. If you can't, say that you can't. Your goal is to *communicate what you feel*, even if you think it will "start something."

Please try to say your feelings out loud. I know you think any normal human should be able to read the non-existent cues you send out, but let's imagine that she does not. I understand you have limited access to your feelings. You are still just a hiker in the emotional wilderness; I understand that. Just do your best. Simply sew together whatever feelings you can. "Meat good." "Face pretty." "Job bad." "Body tired." Whatever it is you can immediately discern and report on, in terms of what is happening inside yourself, say it aloud so she may have a clue as to what you are thinking and feeling. This is the only way she can know you.

She is not a detective, although over the years, she has learned to distinguish between the nonverbal cues you emit. A skin rash equals work pressure. Extra bathroom time means a need for privacy. Eating more means feeling neglected. Sleeping less, internal conflict from financial stress. Whatever the physical manifestations of your emotions, share them with your lady partner. I know you think you *are* sharing them by being in a bad mood or sighing, or yelling about stuff that *isn't* the source of what is really bothering you, but that is not always super clear to women.

A bonus tip: administer physical affection to her without needing it to turn into sex. I understand that this is counter to everything your testes want and your soul comprehends. You see sexual relations as relating, and she sees sexual relations as a culmination of *having related*. But please take my advice, even though it is contrary to your nature. Just take her hand and hold it. Don't put it atop your dick a few seconds later because your physical proximity makes you feel close, which your body equates with sex. She needs this time to feel close to you, even though you are already feeling it. Slow it down, champ. It's the only way she can catch up. Just hold the goddamn hand without the expectation of anything more. Give without desiring to receive. In doing so, in sex and in life, you will eventually get everything you need.

Chapter 5

How to Stop Fighting and Start Fucking

"You wanna avoid a fight with her? Think things you never thought you'd think and say things you never thought you'd say."

The terrifying thing about having a fight with your woman is that you never know how it started. You have stormed out of your own house, keys in hand, with no destination in mind. You have no clue how it devolved to this moment. You were just minding your own business, up there inside your own head—not thinking, talking or communicating in any way. But she's been carrying something around with her all day. She lays it out there for you. You literally don't know how to respond. You take a beat, weighing how best to avoid conflict here. You speak. No matter what you say, it always seems to bounce the wrong way. You feel like there is no right answer to stop this impending war. But there is.

You must remember, not only women's genitals are different from yours: we are different. How we think, talk, and feel are different. We are not the same as you. Feminists have not done women a great service by proclaiming that we are. We're supposed to be gender blind. Post-gender.

And obviously we should be, in things like equal rights, equal pay, and the size of the steaks we eat. But men and women are different. It's not like overly big people, where we're all the same on the inside. We're not. And, sure, yes, physiologically we're not. XX, XY—this is pure science!

But, emotionally, our wiring is totally different, too. In general, you guys are fact based. Women are theorizers. We are feelers. You are doers. We multitask. I observe such gender differences in my own children. I have a son who is ten and a daughter who is seven. When my boy was in kindergarten, I'd ask him daily, so excited to hear every detail, hungry for each morsel, "How was your day?" He'd say, "Good." I'd say, "That's it? That's all? How was it? What did you do? Who did you play with at recess? What was your snack? Were you able to wipe okay?" He'd say, "Great."

So, I had to wait. I waited three years for my daughter to enter kindergarten to find out the answer to this question, "How was your day?" And then she'd launch, like a downhill skier, arms back, tips pointed for speed. There is not enough breath in her lungs. She's like a food binger with words. As soon as my daughter learned to talk, she would not shut up. Sawyer has a thousand tales of her slights: "Stella S. got a bigger pudding!" Her snack: "Pudding! It had a blue cookie on it!" Her indignation: "I tried saying the difference between a hard *g*, 'gah,' and a soft *g*, 'jah,' to Enzo, but he was playing with a train!" Someone she's mad at: "If there's a jail for kids, that's where Hudson should live!" A boy she wants to be friends with, a girl she wishes she wasn't friends with, a jag about a fantastic poop, and a non sequitur about the ending of a book where the giraffe hilariously contracted a case of the hiccoughs.

Don't get me wrong—it's nice to finally hear about kindergarten three years later, but my son as much said the same thing. It was a good day, even great. The composite of these word binges are what make up the difference between how men and women process the same basic experiences. They may arrive at the same conclusion, but men take the shortcut and women take the longcut.

You're Fighting More Because You're Saying Less

It's not that you guys don't feel; you just don't want to share your feelings. You don't have to, because there's no endgame. You don't get anything out of it. In fact, you fear it may only create conflict. That is so much of the reason not to share, because as soon as you do, it gives her the ammunition for something to be contrary about. You will do anything to avoid fighting with her, because to you, it's just a bloodletting of energy. And you truly do not have a map to the land mines, so you avoid the territory entirely. But what if you were actually doing the thing that triggered the fight? What if your silence was the true kindling for her anger? What if you're fighting *more* because you're saying *less*?

Here's a giant fact that you need to memorize about women. (Or you can type it into the "Notes" section on your phone. You may tattoo it on your furry forearm; whatever you have to do to remind yourself.) Here you go:

women think and relate to love and life in a different way than men do. Women want to hear shit out loud. Best example, albeit a familiar one, is February 14's own: "I love you."

You believe that the act of remaining faithful—staple-gunning a loose window screen shut, or wiping a child's shitty bottom—says the exact same thing as "I love you." Maybe it does, to you. These are awful tasks that someone would only do for a person that they absolutely love. BUT, you assume that the emotion can be *inferred* by these acts themselves: "I wipe poo (from the kid that I cocreated, btw); ergo, I love you." $X = Y$, as if feelings were fucking math equations.

I get it, I do—saying it out loud in addition to executing these loving actions feels as redundant and repetitive as saying both "redundant" and "repetitive." But it really does mean a lot to women—an entire group of people who are wired in a different way than you are. No, you wouldn't put gas in an electric car, but you'd be an idiot not to put gas in one that requires gasoline. Women need gas; they need an outward external gesture that expresses your love for them. We need to actually hear the words aloud (or something similar) in order to know you feel them. "Last night he said he loved me. For no reason. (A beat) No, he wasn't coming at the time."

It's the difference between how a woman correlates a special love song to the guy she heard it with, and nostalgizes the romance of that moment, versus the same guy who heard it with her. He may or may not remember that song, but if he does, he will probably associate it as the musical score for the terrific BJ he got that night.

And it doesn't just stop there, either. We women need you not to just say the loving words. We also need you to do the loving things. Right here is the part where you say, "Wait, that's why I stopped at the store on my way home after a very long day to get the milk and those all-important fucking seasonal white peaches. And why didn't she just think ahead to buy diaper wipes? Plus she still wants me to turn the TV off and look her in the eyes while she tells me in tedious detail the world's worst story of a bitch or ass-hole who has it for her at work (who I kind of think may have a good point, but I'd never say so).

And even if I do all of that, she will still say, "When was the last time we kissed? Like, really kissed, and not just before sex. But like the kisses in the beginning just because you loved the way my hair smells? Like you can't help your-self. How come we don't kiss like that anymore?" And then she makes that face. Eyes narrowed and pursed lips; the face of dissatisfaction. You pretend not to get it so you don't have to hear about it more.

You feel judged and criticized. Congratulations! You finally noticed something. You're absolutely right. We *are* judging and criticizing you. Sometimes we do it out loud; sometimes we do it through something called passive-aggression that feels just as bad for you. You may feel, or even say, "Why the hell do I bother making an effort, when all you do is criticize me and tell me that no matter how much I do, nothing is good enough?" You think, "I've just spent so much time listening to her boring story. I gave my opinion on what she needs to do to fix it (this will only make things worse, but you *felt* like you were helping). You say, albeit inside, "I listened for so, so long, taking tiny sips of oxygen, deep life-sustaining breaths to try to stay awake along the way. Then, when I guessed that she finally finished, I go to play a game of Super Hexagon on my phone, and she gets mad at me for disturbing our intimacy. We weren't even fucking! She was talking about a lice infestation in our son's kindergarten class! I can't fix that. So what is the point of even trying?"

Don't Disconnect Too Soon

Let me explain. She felt connected to you, and wanted to remain in that state. But you thought you had already fed her connection, so you felt like you'd earned disconnection. But, and here's the part that is practically genetic: you disconnect at approximately the same frequency that she needs to connect. Just as she was relaxing into your being present for her emotionally ("Yay, he's listening to me! Now, this is what love feels like. I can relax into it."), you were like, "Phew, how the fuck can I get out of here?" This happens especially after sex. She feels very close to you emotionally, but you feel like you could use some space.

But you should really feel badly for me, because I have it far worse. When a woman loves and dates other females, it causes chronic time-consuming emotional conflict. I know you dread spending time in some back-and-forth nattering conversation about emotional dynamics that you could give two shits about. But gay women spend way more time in circuitous blabber, because no one has the genetic coding to remember that most of this stuff isn't important or helpful to discuss. There's no emergency stop valve. Women will literally go around in endless emotional conversation forever, until one of them gets hungry enough or has to pee.

The opposite of this condition is why gay men in relationships have so much sex. They express themselves physically (lotsa fucking!), while women together do a lot of pointless emotional dialoguing (lotsa talking!). Gay men have it so easy. It takes so much less time to take a shower and change the sheets (or not) than it does to get the residue off a really long emotional processing session.

I wish I could tell you that this interactive verbal demonstration of what she considers love to be something that could be avoided. And I hope you have the stomach to read this next bit of truth. *Women will never require less of it.* Sorry to be the bearer of bad news here. But I do assure you that the more you say it, then her search (the nagging, the criticism), the quest for the confirmation of your love will abate. That's the naked economics of supply and demand amongst people of different genders.

Heads up: time spent arguing about what she *doesn't* receive from you will take energy away from any potential for actual sex you may get. Or, even worse, that same time spent *not* having sex with you will become your woman talking to her friends analyzing your actions or inactions. It's a trap. You become your own worst enemy here. As this is the energy she could be expending by giving you a blow job.

Women Analyze Everything

"What the fuck are you talking about?" you may ask. You have no idea about all the emotional dissecting that your wife/girlfriend/lover engages in, but it's so much worse than you could ever imagine. Guess what? However much analysis your woman brings to your attention is *nothing* compared to how much she actually engages in. Fact: Your woman analyzes everything. Her musings about you (and what you do or don't do) isn't just something that she thinks about occasionally. I'm not talking about a small amount of time. Her analysis takes up as much time a day as you spend masturbating, or thinking about the next time you will masturbate.

Women analyze everything. "What did he mean when he said that I look really nice today? Did I not look nice yesterday? Why is he going out of his way to compliment me? What did he do that I don't know about? I'm checking his phone." Or, the converse, "What did he mean when he *didn't* say I looked really nice? I went out of my way to wear those heels he likes that are so fucking uncomfortable. I mean, I got botox injected into my forehead, and he didn't even notice! And if he did notice, that would mean he's aware of my wrinkles and age lines! I'm checking his phone."

And women don't only do this in their relationships with men; they do it with their friendships, as well. If you only knew the kind of elaborate thought processes and fossil explorations we delve into—exploring each nuance of text, call, voice mail, or the absence thereof—you would be completely floored. Men literally have no idea this takes place. Women probe every action and vocalization that people make. They lay them out on a forensic examination table and poke them with a scalpel. You may hear your woman on the phone or her nimble texting fingers running across screens, and be so relieved it isn't directed at you, that you don't wonder what the subject matter is.

Don't be relieved—it *is* about you. Your woman is calling in others for a consult. My friends call me up and ask for a translation: "What did he mean when he said . . . ?" I stick up for you guys, too. I say, he didn't mean anything. At all. Wasn't thinking about it. At all. And if he did, who cares? The moment is over, so why does it matter now? Coming back to it in conversation is only going to make matters worse. He has forgotten. He has zero knowledge of what you're talking about, so move on.

But this won't happen, because it's real to her. So, she will decide to *feel* in a certain way about something she *perceives* you did. Then you come upon her decision regarding your behavior, and it is more dense and complicated than you might ever expect to run into. This is because she has made hard-core assumptions and conclusions. She has maybe even taken a jury poll from several of her friends. She has tried you and hung you, and you never even had a chance to present your side. You didn't know you *had* a side. You were asleep or masturbating, or with the kids, or shitting or playing sports or drinking or working. Then when you come in contact with her, you see that she is "in a mood."

What she really is, is swept up in her conclusions/ convictions. You may wonder, "Why is she acting this way towards me?" You have no clue that she's been rolling around in her perceptions for hours, days, and weeks, building a case against you—based either on something you did, or something she perceives that you did. Remember, men and women digest life differently. After she states her feelings either out loud (anger masks hurt) or by tears (crying *is* hurt), you get defensive. Then you are insensitive. Then you are doubly guilty. And you didn't know any of this was even going on. You just wanted to sit and play a goddamn game on your phone.

Remember: women overanalyze everything, while men aren't usually thinking about anything. Women examine the grooves of a notion. They make assumptions about a certain way you have done something or not done something, and believe it to be the truth. Something else to remember: everything you say and do, a woman takes personally. Everything you *don't* say or do, a woman takes personally.

An example. She went out of her way to buy new sheets. You say nothing. Because you didn't even fucking notice them. Maybe you just felt some abstract pleasant feeling like, oooo, sleep or oooo, sex. But, in her mind, she has a very different narrative. Couple of days ago, she noticed the rubber band thingy on the bottom sheet got ripped up by the dryer and so, even after working for nine hours and saying no to drinks out with her friends, she went to the mall, searched for an elusive parking spot, browsed for almost forty minutes for a new set of sheets, factored you in by dinging several options as too girly, imagined how the one she eventually selected would go with your bed pillows, dealt with traffic, picked up sandwiches for dinner (which bugged you because you prefer a hot meal at night) and finally she crawled into bed, exhausted, and you didn't even mention these nice new blue sheets that—by the way—she also washed. She has had a totally different experience than you. She feels wholly unappreciated and unacknowledged for all that she does every single day.

This is how she handles everything. She fondles it and examines it, even though you're either not clued in or have already moved on to the next thing. It's not her fault; that is just her nature. No matter what you emit or don't emit, she will hoard her tiny projections to form a case against you. This means you're fucked—without ever getting fucked.

To summarize:

- You may go about it differently, but you both want the same thing: to be loved, acknowledged understood, and accepted.

- Hot war, versus cold war. Females want to engage in battle, but males want to tuck in their feelings and be quiet until those feelings fade away. Then you can "get back to normal." You think she just wants to fight, but what she really wants is to engage emotionally. An example: She says, "How come you didn't mention loaning some money to your brother?" You say, "He's paying me back next week. It didn't matter." What this means for her is, "I am a partner here, why wouldn't you just tell me?" What you're saying is, "I don't need to check with you about something I'm handling." To her it's not really about money, it's about feeling included and a part of the process. To you, it never occurred to mention it because you don't need her goddamn permission, plus it was already being dealt with, plus she'd never even know it was gone. But if you offer it up instead, not looking for permission but more as information, it will help her feel included. An emotion that doesn't really register for you. In fact, you'd prefer she wouldn't bother you with this type of boring detail in her life. To her, it speaks to—what else doesn't she know? Point of fact, if you connect and share more often about seemingly innocuous information, your fights will dissipate. You will live in "normal" mode more often.

- Both genders need to be appreciated. Both men and women need acknowledgment of all they do, but women need to hear it said aloud. Men need more of a primal "attaboy"; touch and release is the best method. It's not enough for women just to say, "You're great at being a boyfriend, a spouse, a worker, a dad, provider." Nope, you guys need physical acknowledgment associated with your appreciation. But, if you did say the same type of thing to her aloud—"You're a great girlfriend, wife, mother, worker, caretaker, soup maker . . ." whatever it is you appreciate that you form your lips to acknowledge—she will be so happy you actually said it that she may return the compliment the way you prefer it, with her lips.

If eggshells walked on eggshells, that's how you need to think about the few days right before your woman gets her period. No one wants to talk about this, but indulge me here. Menstruation: the apex of women's gigantic monthly emotions are shed from their precious, exalted hole. The thing you covet the most becomes the thing that grosses you out the most! Women put men through the emotional wringer for three days before our cycle. Also, we never remember that our periods are coming; we never attribute our feelings to being informed by a monthly cycle. We believe, with every fiber of our beings, that our feelings are real, and they exist in the exact measure in which we share them. Women will never admit that these emotions may be souped up, steroid style, from whatever dose of PMS we are on. Our bodies confuse us just as much as we confuse you. And then, just as we are coming down, back from our zone of triple feelings, we bleed from where men want to stick their penises, but now they're just too grossed out. (Bonus information for the men who are not grossed out by our periods: you guys gross *us* out.)

Vagueness Will Be Mistaken for Avoidance

Men and women have different ways of handling things, but the thing that ends up creating the most conflict is the interactive dance we have with each other. For example, women ask about your day because we like to share ours. When you are vague in your response, we assume you have something to hide. We ask too many questions to get to the bottom of things. You feel encroached upon— mistrusted, privacy invaded—and then you are punitive and she is reactive. A fight ensues. Even if she asks the most banal of questions: "Who did you eat lunch with?" "Why are you wearing new underwear?" For you, this can feel like she's a detective trying to ascertain details about your day. You think she is asking you to be accountable, when she just wanted to be included in your routine. Her natural instinct is to share. You intuitively select for more privacy.

Okay, the easy fix here is to give slightly more information to begin with. She will have heard information and communication (the kind she needs to give you), and will feel satisfied. We both only understand our own gender. We assume men are just being shy or shut down, or don't feel like connecting right now, or are hiding things from us. But you're actually just being you. She won't get this, and she never will. So, to avoid this conflict, which you hate more than anything, adapt a little. Give us a shred of something about your day.

She wants to talk about an issue that is bothering her. You would rather light yourself on fire than schedule what you perceive as a later conflict. After all, she's made a point of pinning you down about it; obviously it's something you've done that has upset her. She knows how much you hate these talks, and yet she is doing this again. You anticipate criticism and react accordingly. A fight occurs, which is exactly why you wanted to avoid this conversation in the first place. Ah, but to her, it's the avoidance of this scheduled communication that is creating the conflict.

So the next time she wants to bring up a topic that feels tender for her, say some version of "Okay, let's talk about it now." The fact that you're open to it will throw her off. She will have her topic. It can be something as small as, "Please don't leave your towel on the bed; it makes the sheets moldy." Or something as large as, "I'm not happy." Either way, the more you put it off, the bigger it gets. So, please, deal with it now. If you ignore them, both mold and sadness will grow. It's so much easier to nip them in the bud.

Chapter 6

Cracking the Code
What the Hell Does She Really Want?

"Now act like you like it."

She noisily puts a new roll of toilet paper onto the empty holder with an exasperated sigh. Her pen digs into the grocery list paper as she emphatically writes something down that you just obliviously ate the last of. She wants you to hear her noisy clues. But, the thing is, most of the time you just don't. And if, by random chance, you were focused in on her long enough to clock it, you're not stupid. You're certainly not going to comment on it. "Why are you sighing?" Why would you ask this? You don't ask for the same reason you don't lick your finger and then jam it into an exposed light socket. You tell yourself, "Keep your head down, keep on moving. Clearly you've done something wrong."

All she wants you to do is ask her what's wrong. But you won't. After all, the way her ass just moved when she was angrily jotting down the words "Fruit-at-the-bottom cherry yogurt" has you distracted. Now you're just thinking about her bottom. Or cherries. Or her mouth when she eats yogurt. It's all a jumbly mess to you, but you know you want sex. However, hear this: when you piss off your lady, she's not looking to get fucked out of her bad mood. If you suggest it, or worse, take an *action* to make this happen, she will be pissed off. She doesn't want what you want. You want to fuck away your feelings. That feels nice to *you*. She wants to duke it out emotionally, be acknowledged, validated, and recognized.

To women, feelings are like expensive, rare white truffles. They are so costly, shaved paper thin with a razor to add resonant flavor to everything. To men, these same precious truffles are dirty, shit-coated fungi. Men don't want to talk about this stuff because men have something most women do not have: a sense of goddamned urgency. A driving forward march; a need for emission. They are motivated by the power pack inside their nut sacks. Less talk, more action. Actions always yield more results than theory. It's the fuck-and-make-up approach, versus the find-something-new-to-be-wounded-about method.

The Emotional Reset Button

I'm not saying that women don't have pure, raw sex drives; of course we do. But when a woman is emotionally wounded, we tend not to want to fuck away those feelings, while men love nothing more than doing just that. To guys, fucking is the universal shaking of the Etch A Sketch that returns all things back to square one. It's truly as if men believe our emotional reset button is located deep in the cavity of our vaginas, and the only tool they can use to push it is conveniently attached to them via a tube of skin. "Hmmm. What can I use to get to that reset button, so deep up in there? What do I have handy? Gotta be long enough. Gotta use something that won't get lost when pushed inside. Has to be something solid but with some bend to it, so that I can tap that button effectively. Hmmm, oh I know! This shafty thing between my legs that raises and lowers so well! It's so perfect! It should come attached to me like some kind of Ikea-type Allen wrench fashioned out of epidermis. Oh, wait—it does!"

Well, unfortunately for you guys, this is not where our emotional reset button is located. Finding our button is tough, because there is no one answer as to its location. It's a little like putting a colicky baby to sleep. You must try out a bunch of different things. Soothing, feeding, patting, cuddling, rocking. Not just *one* of these things is always going to work, but most assuredly, a combination of these things will do it. And, eventually, even the fussiest of women will stop crying and nod off to sleep.

So, what do women want? That's about as easy to answer as "How do I make a woman come?" Like hormonally charged thumbprints, no two are alike. There's a general recipe for action, but you people must always be prepared to wear emotional shock absorbers, bending and bouncing left when you were preparing to bounce right.

What Women Never Want to Hear

A few hard and fasts. Here are some things women never want to hear:

Don't ask women about hair removal. Ever. Period. Or our period. Ever. Period.

Don't notice if some weird, oddly located hair has suddenly gone missing. Or if it's where it shouldn't be. This is not the same as not noticing we got our hair cut or blown out, and feeling our wrath at not being noticed after we've gone to some lengths.

Don't notice if our legs are more shaved or less shaved. "Oh! You shaved your legs!" means that every other day, you believe our legs are too hairy. Don't even notice if our pubic hair is almost or entirely absent, or almost or entirely natural. Don't notice any of it. Pretend not to notice if you do. You probably won't notice anyway. Just remember that the following is not a compliment: "Wow, your pubic hair grows really fast!"

Other phrases to avoid:

"Those jeans seem tighter."
"Okay if I skip hanging out with your friends? I
    don't really have anything to say to them."
"You used to be fun/open to it/interested when
    we were first together."
"Something is smelly."

Never say—I mean, *never* say—any version of "Relax/calm down/you're so emotional." "I can't understand you when you're like this." "You're too emotional." "What the hell are you crying about?" "Oh God. Stop crying. Stop it." "I can't listen to the crying." "I can't trust anything that comes out of your mouth four days a month." Any variation of this riff isn't good for you or your penis.

Always Have an Opinion

When we ask your opinion about something that you deem too slight or too who-cares or too why-are-you-bugging me, you still need to come up with an answer. Let's start with the most superficial of all stereotypical examples. When she asks you which type of shoe you prefer—"This one or this one . . . ? This? Or this?"—please do not say, "I don't see the difference." Even if that *is* your true opinion, you still may not say it. (Of course women have other interests than what shoes we wear on our feet. I might've said, "Which physics degree places a greater emphasis on the exploration of thermodynamics?" But for simplicity's sake, let's just go with this one.)

Instead, pick a position. Here's a secret about her: when she asks you which shoe you prefer, she already has a favorite. Please proceed here with terrific caution; this is a mind ambush. She wants her opinion echoed. She wants to be agreed with. *This is a trap.* So your opinion has to be an expansive one. Either agree with whatever she's not saying out loud, or have a different opinion that makes better sense than the one she's already surreptitiously chosen. If she's asking you, it means she doesn't want to hear the very Swiss-sounding middle-of-the-tepid-road "I like the one *you* like." This will not fool or appease her. This means you're not listening, and you're a spineless dick. This will only piss her off. Angry heat will radiate off her. Why did she bother opening her mouth to ask you in the first place?

So even if your opinion is "I don't give a shit," or "Can't you see I'm thinking about a stupid mistake I made at work?" or "When was the last time I ate an apple?" or "Gasket!" Or "I miss all the women I'm not banging because I made a stupid vow to you. But that's not enough; you're still asking me about your idiotic shoes! Who cares! They're just something you put on your feet!" No matter what your opinion really is, you must formulate a reasonably intelligent one. So instead, say, "I like the black ones." Let's say, in her head, she's already picked out the navy ones. So your opinion, even though you don't care at all, must be well thought out enough for her to believe that you care. The most heinous of crimes is not having an opinion. It means you don't care. And if you don't *care*—which you probably don't—it implies that you don't care *about her*. Wait. How did she make that crazy leap? But she does. I know this doesn't make sense to you. But to her, not having an opinion about the color of her shoes means you don't love her.

Told you we were complicated. So, just like the penis you'd prefer to shove down her throat, put your opinion there instead. Choose it. Stick to it. You say, "I like both, but if I really had to pick one, I'd say the black ones because they look good with the rest of your outfit, but they also remind me of the last time you wore them." (Just bullshit your way through this; I know you don't remember at all.)

"I don't know where we went, I just remember laughing a lot that night and thinking I was lucky to be with someone I love spending time with. Then I checked out your legs and thought they were extra sexy, so I made a mental note of the shoes you were wearing: the black ones." Now, she can't be mad at this, even if they're not the shoes she originally, secretly wanted you to pick. You answered thoughtfully. You made it personal. You even loogied up a little morsel of something more; something yearning and emotional. And, if for some reason you didn't get the answer right, there never was a right answer.

Never Talk about Your Ex(es)

Another tip: *don't compare your exes.* "When I was with Francesca, she used to make me pull over to have sex with her on the side of the road. She couldn't go more than a day without me inside her. But you're not like that." "When Desiree and I were together, she let me toe-bang her." "One time in college, a girl, can't remember her name . . . gave me a hand job at the library. I came on the books. I miss doing stuff like that." Never discuss your exes. Especially in bed. She doesn't want to imagine that your penis has ever been inside anyone or anything but her. (Unless she *wants* to imagine it inside someone else—and that's, like, her thing.) But the rule here is that you should pretend your dick is a freshly forged sword; newly poured steel. Never before touched by human hand, much less sword-swallowed.

It's like when you move into a new house or apartment, and want to replace the toilet seat. You don't want the ghost of asses having shat there before. Even more so, she doesn't ever want to think about your penis (as in *her* penis) inside someone else. You can't scour off the memories of where it's been with steel wool, but you can certainly not discuss them. Your dick must be like a brand new toilet seat. If your sexual history ever comes up, just don't remember anyone else, even though I know you replay them all, including the ones you haven't even had, as you sploop inside her.

～

I know you want to ask her, but don't. "How many guys have you been with?" Men definitely want to know their partner is wanted by other guys, but you also want to believe that she desires only you. This is a very double-edged skin sword because you want to imagine your woman is gorgeous and interesting enough to be desired by many, but you don't actually want to think about or hear the brush-stroke details of her fucking anyone but you. It's sexy until it's something you can never unknow.

There's also a terrifying moment between the question and the answer where you're not sure if your level of sexual experience matches hers. You don't want to be the guy who fucked six women, only to find out your fiancée's sexual track record is vast. I guess some guys like to hear about their woman's sexploits, but if they become too many and much ("He was so big, he couldn't even fit the whole thing inside me . . . I mean, we tried . . ." "He made me bend over his Ferrari . . ." "We did it backstage at the Hollywood Bowl after his performance . . .") . . . You get it. There's this one central area in her body where all these dicks have undoubtedly hung out before you; it's like the VIP room of her insides. Your dick is in the exact same place as his and his and his was. So don't even start up this mental discomfort by asking. It's not worth it.

But do be ready to answer the question if she asks you. If your number is overwhelming, it will not impress her; it will just gross her out. That means your penis has no standards. If your number is underwhelming, we won't think your demi-virginity is adorable. We will want you to already have worked out your kinks on someone other than us. Basic tip: just don't ask, unless you're certain you can deal with any answer that comes out of her mouth—and the truth won't distract you the next time you're coming in her mouth.

It's basic economics: most of us want the item that is highly valued and therefore sparse, nearing the bottom of the chafing dish on the buffet table. Far fewer of us want what others reject; the weird surplus of runny mayonnaisey raisiny carroty salad congealing in abundance.

Women Are Easily Bored

Women want stability, but are also very easily bored. These two feelings fight each other, but both are true. It's the same for you guys; if you get too complacent, you lose interest. It's like when a hunter's prey just submits itself to be eaten ("the suicidal chicken"), then that food is way less tasty. Half the fun in the licking of the bones is procuring it, and knowing the value of how hard you've worked to obtain it.

Some of you actually believe the rule of "The hotter the female, the worse you're supposed to treat her." You're using the theory that if you treat her like shit, she will think she only deserves the love of a dickhead like you. Sure, you can take advantage of a woman who was emotionally or physically victimized earlier in life, and believes that she doesn't deserve better. Your bad behavior will certainly intrigue these already complicated, broken creatures. Between treatments that place too much emphasis on her physical beauty (ombre dye jobs, invasive cosmetic surgeries and collagen injections, etc.), she may wonder, "Why isn't this man treating me like a princess, the way all other men have always treated me?" This may momentarily snag and captivate her.

The too-pretty woman walks through a world of cocktails purchased for her, and great valet parking spaces. This isn't some urban legend. It is way better to be super beautiful—even though it comes with its own set of tough, albeit Vuitton, baggage. While the theory of treating someone like shit may occasionally work with a sexy coke-snorter in the short term, it is impossible to get what you actually want/need from her in the long term. Unless what you want is hostility, neediness, and her leaving you for someone else.

So, be nice. Be kind. While women may want a bad boy occasionally, dating a true asshole will only make her realize she needs someone who is not an asshole. The asshole becomes the barometer for all men thereafter, and paves the way for her to meet an actual nice guy. You often hear about a woman being in a long-term relationship with an asshole, and then finally gathering enough courage to end it, only to meet and quickly marry someone great. The reason for this is because the asshole has spent years being what she doesn't want in a person, so after him, it's easy to identify a desirable partner.

Are you a nice guy? The answer doesn't have to be yes. Some of you just aren't ready to commit. And then, suddenly, you are; it's when you realize that it would be more intolerable to let that woman go than to lock her down for a lifetime. Some guys meet that person right out of the gate, and they're good forever. And some are always on that quest, whether in a relationship or not.

(Obviously some women aren't ready to commit, either. So don't pounce on me for not including women in the above sentence. Everyone's so testy these days, eager to assassinate and deconstruct every position. Twitter has ruined personal points of view for everyone. I'm scared to admit any unpopular or off-popular opinions for fear of being publicly lashed. Like, okay, sometimes, I miss getting plastic bags at the grocery store. Okay, assholes, go for it! Everybody pile on and yell at me about my environmental shortsightedness! I just need something to stick a kid's wet bathing suit in!)

Women Want to Let Go of Control

So, you all can get ready to ball up your fists when I say that *all bad boys aren't bad*. As I mentioned before, most women want a little throw-down. Of course I'm not talking about physical violence or verbal abuse in any way or shape. Just some light caveman shit here. One of the bestselling books of all time is the even newer testament *Fifty Shades of Grey*. I will admit to sneaky Kindle plane-reading it.

But a woman needs to be reminded to let go of control. Moms with jobs are "working moms," while dads with jobs are just "dads." Mothers never ever clock out. We are constantly puppeting our kids with verbal instructions: "Don't drag that! Stop, it's leaving marks." "Pick up your underpants and put them where they're supposed to go. No, not there. No. No. The hamper. No. That's not a hamper." "Please stop sharing that story if chicken or macaroni is going to fall out of your mouth during the telling. No, it doesn't make a difference if it's chicken *and* macaroni."

A woman is instructive/caring/bossy in arduous and exhaustive repetition. Dante's unmentioned Tenth Circle of Hell is the nagging associated with motherhood and wife-life. But she isn't doing it to be annoying and grating, or to conjure up images of your own mother. She is controlling because she feels that her way of doing things is correct. Truth: she can't imagine being any other way. And, if for some reason she's not saying anything to you about the way you're doing something, it's because she is either bit-ing her goddamned tongue or for some far more rare reason: that she imagines your way of doing it has inadvertently coincided with the way she would've done it.

Someone needs to stop this ongoing Morse code of instructions on how to live life. That's why we went out in droves and bought tons of copies of *Fifty Shades* of no fucking shit. Christian Grey was doing what we all occasionally need done. The handsome, rich, sexy caretaker was going to do just that. Some women need this mental permission to take a break. Most just need to read about it, or even hear some version of it whispered to them while fucking, without actually participating in real bondage. A woman needs permission to shut off her brain. A hundred million copies would most decidedly agree: a wave of people are relating to this in a big way.

This best-selling book of all time went on to become one of the biggest movie openings of all time. Proving, when people aren't actually fucking, they love to read about fucking or watch other people fucking. People are really into fucking.

In overwhelming numbers, women want permission to give up control in some arena. Yes, sure, in the bedroom, too. Despite huge careers and motherhood and wifehood, women also want to have the option *not* to be liberated— even if it is just for eleven minutes a day. They want to relax a little, be taken out of their heads, be taken care of for a change. They want to stop all the list-making noises inside. Stop all the planning and noodging. Sometimes they can't do it all by themselves, and that requires someone else to take over. And not just with sex. It is not fashionable to acknowledge that women need to be jarred from their mental to-do lists with an occasional sexy arm squeeze and/or light ass-smack. Women have and will work hard for equality, but we haven't evolved so far that we don't also still want to be taken care of sometimes . . . even if it's only about half as much as we're taking care of others.

Women don't volunteer to feel this way; they need to be cajoled, distracted from their own heads. Christian Grey, that coiffed and humorless white dude, does it with cuffs and/or paddles. That's probably too extreme for most, but the underlying emotional issue is still the same: "Take me out of my brain that instinctively nests and caretakes and mothers, worries and obsesses and takes care of you, too, in a thousand ways, large and small. *Force* me to be taken care of."

This is a woman's wiring. Do you know how much more pussy you would get if you took three seconds when you got home to grab your woman from behind, kiss her neck, tell her she looks hot with that makeshift ponytail of unwashed hair, and tell her she's going to get it later? And, if you throw down a sack of Thai food on the counter to punctuate that notion, well, you don't need to hear from me how much fucking you'll get. Odds are, your dick is still wet.

So be sure to be in charge sometimes. I know, all this seems like a lot to have to do. Ugh, no one wants to go out and buy handcuffs or a cowboy handkerchief. Just seems like another to-do on your already endless list of chores.

This is emotional dominance more than physical. It's you taking charge, handling little details and giving her head a break from its constant whirr.

The Grown-up Version of the Gold Sticker

If you'd like to step yourself up to a new sexual plateau, there are so many tiny things you can do to improve your general sexual status. I mean, you work your ass off at Candy Crush, and no one's going to blow you when you matriculate to the next level. In fact, if you boast to her about it, this thing you've worked so hard to accomplish, she will be so annoyed about the time you wasted on it and not on her or the kids or your lives together.

Wait, hang on, you were just clearing your head, zoning out—but to her, it's another thing that is soaking up attention from her. Your game is like an electronic hooker stealing your time, attention, money, and fidelity of spirit. You're a smart man. You live for the reward system. You love getting a promotion at work, or back in your childhood when your kindergarten teacher used to put a gold sticker on your test. Think about how hard you worked to earn those. It said, "Nice job." This is how you should think about yourself and your relationship. There is a very simple reward system for your thoughtfulness in life. Let's call it the "blow job gold sticker." If you work extra hard, you will be rewarded as an adult, too.

Here are just a few small suggestions of things you can do to accrue quick and easy points that will add up to more fucking for you, but this list is by no means definitive; it is a constantly moving target only as small as your imagination or your desire to fuck.

- Put away your phone and listen.
- Ask about her mother.
- Listen when she tells you about her mother.
- Make a reservation for Valentine's Day way in advance, at a restaurant only she likes.
- Remember the kind of ice cream she loves best. Buy two pints. Eat neither.
- Offer to rub her back. While doing it, don't attempt to rub her front.
- Plug in her phone when you notice she is low on battery.
- Take her dry cleaning in. Remember to pick it up.
- Make the bed.
- Remind your child to make his or her bed.
- Clean out the fridge of all the disgusting, old, outdated, and moldy things.
- Buy all new condiments for the fridge.
- Compliment something about her that you really don't like.
- Offer to work on something about yourself that she really dislikes.
- Get her a new umbrella and have it ready for when it rains. Yes, this is a metaphor of pre-

paredness and protectiveness. She'll see it that way, too.

- Send her a nonsexual selfie or video. It means you're thinking about her when she's not there.
- Text her just because you miss her, and not only when you want to remind her to do something for you.
- Write her an actual note on an actual piece of paper.
- Purchase something new for the house that she saw and wanted, but didn't buy.
- Like her parents.
- Offer to get together with her parents.
- Don't subject her to your own parents.
- Like her friends.
- Offer to hang out with her friends.
- Don't subject her to your own friends.
- On the off chance that you ever let her drive, keep your opinions about the route she's chosen to yourself unless she asks.
- Out of the blue, mention some small thing she did and say how grateful you are that she did it.
- Take your kids out for the afternoon without being asked.
- Take your dog to the groomer without being asked.

- Take her car in to be serviced, and deal with the to-and-from the shop all by yourself.
- Kiss her between her shoulder blades.
- Make out with her vagina.
- Clean the gutters.
- Hold her hand.
- Call her your girlfriend, even though she's your wife.
- Brag about her to her girlfriends; it will get back to her.
- Stop her with a compliment about something that's not about how she looks physically.
- If you notice that she's lost weight or gained it, don't say anything either way. Instead, grab her by the waist and kiss her gently on the mouth. That's it. That's your woman, and that's the size she comes in. The kiss is your stamp of approval.
- Cook something for her or clean up something that she cooked for you.
- Volunteer to provide whatever idiotic thing your kid's school wants for the teacher appreciation day.
- Be in charge of something, anything, and follow through with it.
- Notice something that is broken around the house all by yourself. Either fix it or have it fixed without being asked.

- Order a jacket she doesn't know about and wear it on a date you ask her to go on.
- Pretend to be on a first date together.
- Or, even better, pretend it's your first date and you haven't fucked her yet. Don't tell her you are doing this. You will act as interested as you pretended to be the first time.

She won't even know this is all adding up to sex. She will think you're being generous with your time, paying attention to her and to others. She will feel like she has some weight lifted off her shoulders. All this will allow for some time to entertain the notion of sex. You will be rewarded, and she will feel as though she is really rewarding herself.

Exhausting, right? All of this will probably make you want to throw in the towel. But imagine what your life would look like without her, or some other version of her in your life. Seems fun for a few days or even a month, but then there's you alone, living with a hand-crank can opener and spooning a can of who-cares-what into your mouth. That's you all by yourself, doing whatever you want with your computer, never having to remember to clear your history. That's you with an economy-sized container of lotion with a pump dispenser and a giant flu season–sized box of Kleenex. So what if you occasionally have to make an extra effort to march double-time? It will ultimately be more fruitful in the struggle for lifetime happiness.

When you understand what a woman actually wants, it's worth it because you share a true emotional connection. Plus you get laid. But whether you understand this actively or not, she *is* the receptacle for all of your desires, even if you sometimes confuse them for just the ones associated with your penis.

Chapter 7

The 21st Century Female

"I guess you didn't get my text."

I just downloaded a new operating system to my phone, only because the little numeral circly thingy on it wouldn't disappear. It nagged at me visually, like a text I hadn't yet checked. And after my free and painless download, it really has the phone looking so much prettier. It came up with a whole new way of doing things that I never would've guessed, or even knew to need. And it did it so thoughtfully, without me ever imagining I'd want this stuff. It took care of me. This phone is my very diligent lover, anticipating needs I didn't even know I *should* have.

But as with any relationship, there are always tiny drawbacks. Now the whole thing has slowed down so much, I feel like I have to go out and buy the next generation of it. So I go out to buy the new phone. (If you're the one asking why I didn't just buy it online, then you're part of the problem.) It's a good thing I went to the mall, too, because I can buy anything from a computerized kiosk now. It doesn't smell like a bakery, but I can have a cupcake at the push of a button; no need for human contact or its endless bad cologne choices. Which is also good because of the transmission of airborne illnesses, plus stuff like having to make irritating small talk, which I like less and less because I could be checking Twitter or Instagram during life's inconvenient pauses.

But when I finally get to the Apple store, there are all these other new and next things, all because I clicked the little numeral update thingy. Now I have to go buy a bunch of other stuff because they've changed the way the newer phone plugs in. More prongs or fewer prongs, which will charge me up faster and juicier. Now I need a new car adapter and a bedside charger and a charger for work and a backup charger and a bonus battery-powered adapter, you know, just in case I need to Vine a video of a hike I'll never take. Oh, yeah, I also need a new sturdy but ironic says-something-about-me protective case for my larger and faster, but certainly differently shaped phone. When I get home, I put all my old tech stuff in a drawer. And as I do, it hits me that the idea behind faster, newer, better, upgradable, toss-it-away, Adderall-fueled technology can be applied to our sex lives and relationship attention spans.

See, bitches? This *did* have something to do with fucking. And, by the way, I still haven't upgraded my phone. They didn't have any in stock, those back-ordered teasing motherfuckers. Plus, my contract wasn't up.

My kids don't believe me when I tell them that when I grew up . . . "I walked three miles to school every day in the snow, without shoes." No, but I do boast of my own agonizing bootstraps: "There was no pause button on my TV remote." However, they don't even look up as I say this. Why would they? Their eyes are stuck on their various iPads, LeapFrogs, or, if I'm lucky, Kindles. I continue, "Yes, I know it sounds crazy, but it's true. When the commercials came on, my whole family would shove each other out of the way to grab a snack or be the first one to get to the bathroom!" My kids still manage to make me feel stupid as they ask in dismissive unison, "Why didn't you just watch it on your phone?"

Yearning Is Sexy

When did this happen? When did it all just get to be too much? Do we think that our sexual relationships haven't been dramatically altered by this whole new technoscape? And forget about masturbation. As long as there have been hands, there have been people looking at objects and faces and lumps and curves and creases of genitals in various degrees and rearranging them in some new and imaginary way in order to self-stimulate.

The JCPenney catalogue used to be a sperm-coated mess. *National Geographic?* Men somehow managed to look past the distended bellies of a starving population of women to objectify their indigenously necklaced tits. But at least guys back then had to use their imaginations to some degree. They actively had to picture what the peri-menopausal models in a catalogue might look like without their flammable underpants on. Did she have a big bush?

A little bush? *No* bush? The imagination required to think of these questions all served as the backbeat to the front-beat. The curiosity cultivated a need for human interaction that we no longer have.

We no longer have to imagine what breasts look like without the benefit of a Sears, Roebuck and Company brassiere, the way your grandpa did, hunched out of sight from your grandma inside his rusty and warped toolshed. Nope, now there are free vaginas everywhere to jack off to. In more recent decades, boys would have to sneak their parents' VCR copy of *Fast Times at Ridgemont High* in order to fast-forward and freeze on Phoebe Cates's perky boobs as she removed her bikini top in diabolically timed slo-mo. They would watch *Basic Instinct*, craning to snag a glimpse of Sharon Stone's are-they-really-blond vagina lips as she crossed and uncrossed her panty-free legs under her microskirt.

But now, forget it. It's so easy; too easy. Any person can search for any version of women's private parts imaginable. All they have to do is memorize what birth year alleges they're "Safe to Enter" and then, without the slightest hint of proof, boom, there they are: bountiful vaginal bouquets. We can look at any version of any vagina at any time, at no cost other than to self. We can have a twenty-four-hour-a-day, seven-day-a-week all-access pussy pass (including all the endless unpronounceable Jewish holidays) for a front row seat to any crazy and rare anything and everything. I guess postmillennial imagination is a new kind of muscle, one that only requires that we dream it in order to find it. Any vagina, any tits, no oddity too big to conjure. "May I see a hound's-tooth vagina?" No thank-you is required.

Congratulations on being born when you were, because men for generations had to jerk off to fig. 1171 from *Gray's Anatomy*. (You are searching for this image right now.) In our on-demand society, where is the *want*? *Want* is that unfulfilled piece where yearning is born. That yearning is sexy. Looking forward to something we can't immediately access is what creates desire. Desire creates urge. Urge creates action. Action creates connection. Connection is when people meet. When people meet, they can love and/or fuck. If they love and/or fuck, life is possible. What happens to us without all that? End times. Sigh.

Never Send a Picture of Your Penis

There are so many apps for secret-style fucking now. Apps and websites dedicated to people who are looking to have affairs. But, beware, as convenient as they are for hooking up, that same technology can also get you busted. Snoopy spouses can search stuff to get clues about what you're doing in private. There are even apps like Couple Tracker or mSpy or Find My Kids that she can download onto your phone to track where you are, versus where you *say* you are. Gone are the days of just walking in on someone fucking someone else. Ironically, technology will probably end more relationships than ever before, because there are so many more ways to find out if someone is lying to you about the women he's secretly met while technologically hooking up.

Okay, super-big point here with photo sexting: DO NOT SEND A PHOTO OF YOUR GENITALS, EVER. Your genitals are called "private parts" for a reason. It just is never a good idea. Even in a moment of testosterone-fueled bad decision-making, it is as forever as the memory of Anthony Weiner's political career.

Also, less discussed than the forever quality of owning the image of someone's dick pic is the new age-old question, "What the hell are women supposed to do with this photograph?" If you're kind of a stranger, we don't want to see your dick unless we're checking for quality. If you are our boyfriend, someday we could get mad at you and send it to all our friends; show them how short, tall, big, or small, or how extreme your bend to the left is. A photo is forever, and easily forwarded. So just don't take it to begin with. It can never be unsent.

But, if you're not going to listen to me, and you feel like you MUST take a pic of your turgid weenie for some girl you're sexting with, *do not ever include your face in the same shot as your cock.* Do not include any identifiable tattoos or incriminating background locations, moles or spots that indicate that this dick is your dick. Imagine your penis walking in a perp lineup. Don't let it be ID'd. This is some very good advice; please take it.

It's Delishy

So I'm engaged for the first time in my life. Maybe as you read this, I'll already be legally married. All a sort of fantastical series of words mashed together to form a sentence I never would've thought possible. Who knew that, as a gay woman, I'd ever enjoy the same privileges granted to other couples?

Well, technology plays a part in how I met Liz, my fiancée. But if technology could be thought of as old-fashioned, that's the typing type we enjoyed. A mutual friend introduced us and it began; certainly slowly, a Duggar-like courtship of endless back and forth texting. We got to know every detail about each other before ever going out on a single date. We never even spoke on the phone.

As we texted for months, we let each other in on whatever moment-by-moment feeling we were having in real text time. These late-night text sessions were rife with unveiled emotional intimacy. No, not the kind you'd think. Not a single sexy text was exchanged but, instead, moments of real vulnerability. It felt even more intimate than the more garden variety "Whatcha wearing . . .?" sexy-type typing.

The result was that when we actually went on a real face-to-face date, I felt way too emotionally exposed. Drowning in how much she knew about me, not able to pull down those safe-feeling facades as easily. It was too late. I had texted the truth about self and soul with her already. It's a far more nebulous closeness. It takes less courage to type out your vulnerable insides to a disembodied numerical face than expose yourself by sharing with an actual human being. Inserting a crying emoticon really isn't the same as shedding a tear. But Liz and I got to know each other in these lengthy text sessions that filled up the crevices of our own lives. I had the opportunity to be more open about myself than I ever would've dared risking in real life.

So, of course, when we actually sat down for sushi, the result was a meltdown for me. An imbalanced equilibrium of her already knowing me, versus me feeling overexposed in person. Not a great first date. I got out of there fast. I was in the parking lot of the restaurant when I texted my wise friend, Jenni (because all women communicate every god-damned emotional shred, including lesbians . . .). I told Jenni, "No. Not going to happen." Me, incredulous: "She used the word 'delishy' to describe a crab hand roll." Jenni yelled at me for being the word police. Liz and I went out again without the overwhelming emotional meltdown of it being the first time. Happily ever after. Liz still says "del-ishy." Maybe a little less than she used to. And of course it bugs me, it's "delishy"—but she is who she is, so the only way for me to have a happy relationship is to accept her.

The Rules for Texting

But here's the thing: although texting can be a very helpful tool to learn more about each other, it can never replace actual human connection. Texting is connection on ste-roids. A text demands your attention; it doesn't care what you're doing in that moment—it says, "Pay attention to me!" It can become wholly sexual—sexting to fruition—which can emulate intimacy. It can even begin to imitate a real relationship and then, when you're together in real life, it can suddenly feel alienating and unfamiliar. Not the true connection of what you've experienced together before. It's as if the bond you shared was about the size of your iPhone.

And men and women interrelate differently even with technology. Women examine every nuance of every conversation. This is also true with anything technological. The modern age affects women's obsessional qualities, as well. My friend's eighteen-year-old daughter came to me for advice about a new boy she was dating. Taylor, all flustered and maddened: "He hasn't *liked* any of my Instagrams at all. And he didn't comment or even reply-all about my 'Boo, the world's cutest Pomeranian getting groomed' video that I sent him and eighteen of my other friends."

That is modern anything-but-love. The "rules" of dating can't even be applied anymore. How long to wait to return someone's text? There's no "Wait a couple days to return his call." Or "Don't fuck him until the third date." There isn't even a *first* date. The young just hook up at group gatherings. Everything moves so fast. Young women click and dispatch before thinking anything through, and then he's already cc'd all and forwarded a random batch of boys your innermost thoughts and thighs that an uncontrolled mass of people can save on a cloud just for the short time of *forever*.

There's always a new app, a new jolt of what feels like connection in under 140 characters—always wanting permission to use your current location. And FaceTime, wow. So intrusive. Nothing moves slowly enough not to return calls. Taylor composed six versions of a text to connect to a tanned, toned swim team boy who lanced her virginity on a hook up. "Do I exclaim, or use ellipses . . .?!" Each dot was thunk over as if it was the actual debate to lose her virginity—which incidentally, she dispatched within the time it took to press send.

I assured her that wherever the swimmer was the night we debated and agonized over punctuation marks, he was not somewhere composing theoretical lists of possible texts to send to her. Different pitches with various "What's up?" "Wassup . . . . ?" "Where r u??" "Where r you . . . ?" "U around?" "You around . . . ?" No, he was actually out there in life, stalking, claiming, masturbating to, or discussing pussy. The swimmer was either almost fucking someone or actually fucking someone, or asleep after having fucked someone. A blissfully empty sac, agitation juice relieved.

This isn't to say that the gorgeous, brilliant, superbrainy Taylor gave something up to him that she didn't want to give. She gave it willingly and wantingly. She confided to me that she thought this swim guy was a little stupid. The ironic "Communications" major. But that she was really into hanging out with him again. When I asked her what she thought they'd do if they were to hang out again, she shyly admitted she was thinking about the sex. I asked if she was looking for the connection part, the intimacy? "No," she admitted, all blushily. They couldn't really connect, she explained, because he wasn't intellectually stimulating enough to scratch that itch for her. She was only really interested in the physical/sexual connection, but her body and her feelings *still read* his abject disinterest as unfulfilled yearning and rejection.

Poor Taylor. Really, she just wanted to objectify the swimmer as much as he wanted to objectify her. She only wanted to fuck him, but she still registered his disappearance as a wound, when all she wanted was the same thing he did. That's the gender difference manifested: they were both using each other, but her lady feelings still perceived his disappearance as emotionally injurious.

The Fast Food Theory

Do you know that guy who loves to have sex with any woman he can? I'm sure the answer to you is, "Yes, all men do." But I actually have a theory about this type; the ones who just can't help themselves. This is certainly not helped by the Internet with all its magical portals and ways to meet new people. Men who sleep with a whole bunch of women, versus those who only sleep with a select few. I call it the Fast Food Theory: a burger chain has filled the bellies of literally billions, but does not provide a very good meal nutritionally. Though delicious in the moment, it usually leaves you with a desire for something more substantive.

You're filled with a salty regret. But, if you spend a little more time picking and preparing your food, you and your body will feel healthier.

I wanted to ask someone who would have an opinion on this. I wanted to talk to someone who has tested out my theory. Someone who had been fucking women long before I started, and continues to do so long after I confined my options to just the one. So I went out to dinner with John Stamos. You know the guy I'm talking about: the coyly smirking guy with excellent hair from *Bye Bye Birdie* on Broadway. Before that, he was John, the guy with excellent hair on *Glee,* or Tony the excellent-haired paramedic on NBC's *ER.* Long before that, he was the nineties excellent-haired Uncle Jessie on ABC's *Full House.* Before that, he was the eighties Blackie "excellent hair" Parrish on ABC's *General Hospital.* He was on a show that I cocreated with Ryan Murphy, NBC's *The New Normal.* What I didn't confess to John while we were working together was that I possessed a lifelong *Tiger Beat* crush that superseded all lines of sexuality.

See, John Stamos is the universal donor. We humans are all attracted to John, regardless of our collective sexuality. Stamos is a staple in any writers' room as "a theoretical guy." A Theoretical Guy is a person of fantastic charm and handsomeness that another (usually less-attractive straight) man must allow for the possibility of having a sexual encounter with. A "but-what-if-that-man-was-John-Stamos" heterosexuality barometer.

Me: "Really? Your dick's never moved for any man, ever?" Sample straight man: "No. Nope. Not into it." Me: "Okay, so no one? There's not a man alive you ever remotely could get a boner for?" Sample man: "It's not a homophobic thing, just not into it." Me: "Okay, I get it. You're so straight; you wouldn't take a free and easy blow job? No conversation required afterwards. No compliments or thank-you necessary. Just unpause the *Daily Show* and drift off to sleep."

I can tell this scenario appeals in some way to Sample Straight Man, never having really had it so articulated before, because now there is a dawning realization. "Ohh. No, I don't think so, no." Me: "So just like, theoretically, what if some dude bought you a Porsche just because he thought you were cool, adamantly agreed that your dad had unrealistic expectations of you, and laughed aloud at all of your jokes, even your stupid puns. He made you feel special . . ." Sample Straight Man wanes, considering: "What kind of Porsche? Not, like, a Boxster?" Me, knowing I have him in my sights now: "No man alive? Not even, like, John Stamos?"

Okay, now we're in the zone. This is where even straight men must allow for the possibility of a theoretical Stamos blow job: "I mean, if my eyes were closed . . . guess it could be anybody's mouth, right? I could pretend it was a woman's mouth. I mean, John *is* very good looking. (Then, getting into it . . .) Bet he's had so many BJs, he'd be very good at it."

John is also the great lesbian equalizer. I wanted to sleep with him, too. Who am I to be immune to his ridiculous adorableness? John is how pretty I require my men to be. It's why I become straight for four-hour pockets, every dozen years, give or take. So absurdly handsome, he's almost a well-kempt butchy female. But pop culture pedigree aside, I was hypnotized by him. I'm sure it had something to do with his fame, as with any attraction to anything excellent, but what he emits is way more than a garden-variety case of star fuck. His twinkly-eyed Greekness, the self-confidence associated with a lush thicket of hair are impossible to ignore. I never actually had the chance to sleep with John, because in the time between working with him and actually wanting to have sex with him, I found and fell in love with my person. So, Stamos case closed. But it didn't stop me from eating a steak with someone who's as good an actor as he is a friend.

We met at the Palms in Beverly Hills. I wanted us to sit underneath his own caricature. Without even asking, he ordered for me and my girlfriend. King crab meat appetizer. Coupla steaks. Cheesy potatoes. Creamed spinach. For himself, he chastely got a simple fish with a monkish squeeze of lemon. He was interrupted no less than four times for photos, and every time he smiled and happily posed as if it was the first time in his life to ever be asked. Between interruptions that seemed to annoy only me, he asked what I was working on. I told him about the book. I laughed between bites of the heavenly quadruple potato cheesy thing he'd ordered and said, "I should probably interview you. You have so much experience."

"I don't know," he said. "I might not be that good at it. I could probably use the tips."

Wow, wait. John's penis had been inside maybe a tenth of the Screen Actors Guild, and here he was, admitting possible ignorance. Beyond the hair, the money, the sex appeal, the in-through-the-out-door ride entrances at Disneyland—here he was, confidently admitting that he didn't know everything. No wonder this guy got laid so much!

Steal from his wisdom: When you openly admit gaps of knowledge, it makes someone want to teach you something while being simultaneously open to your not being excellent at it. Acknowledging imperfection allows for a learning curve and degrees of improvement. As I type this, I am only right now realizing that maybe I'd been played. Did I fall for John's brilliant method of feigned ignorance, or was he being guileless? Not that it mattered; his modesty alongside his ability to de-pants someone with his dimpled, flirty smirk was a walloping duo.

Wisdom from an Expert

So in wanting to talk to John further about this book, I met him again for breakfast. Of course he ordered feta in his egg-white omelet. As I described the topic of the book, how to fuck a woman, he volunteered:

John: I am the last expert on the planet. But first and foremost, it's respect. I want her to be turned on and be happy ten times before I even get off even once. I have an ego that the woman's takeaway is, "Wow, he was great in bed, what a piece of ass Stamos is," and she wins because I put all my energy into whatever turns her on.

Ali: So, wait, is that ego (which is inside you) or reputation (which is things people say about you)? I mean, if you were a less attractive person, less famous, would you feel the same?

John: I guess, it's not funny or anything but the truth is—I care. I think it's about body communication. Listening to her. I always feel like I talk too much about myself in life. So, I want to ask a million questions of her. It's just more interesting when you know someone. Same thing with her body.

Ali: But, you're you. Don't you automatically get the girl? What's the challenge?

John: People think that. I don't know what it's like not to be me, but I'm not the Lothario everyone thinks. I haven't had sex, like intercourse, in a year because I'm at that point in my life where I don't want to give shit away.

Ali: Aren't you sort of quantifying your experiences (my Bill Clinton theory) with the intercourse version of sexual experience being the only one? Could it be that orgasm (or at least the valiant attempt to get it) should be the definition, not penetration?

John nods, absorbing this.

Ali: I wonder if you don't "give it away" because of supply and demand? Like, you've had such a wealth of women, maybe it matters less to you?

John: I'm fifty-one years old. I've had some experience but it's about listening, asking, talking . . . Maybe some girls are afraid of communicating. But I find most aren't if you ask, "Does this feel good?" Or listen to her body like an instrument. (This coming from the guy who occasionally plays drums with the Beach Boys.) I guess I do approach sex in a musical way. With me, it's more rhythm than melody with a woman . . . but it's all listening. When music clicks, you can feel it. You have to listen to the other musicians. With women, you have to listen to their bodies. Not just listen to them say out loud, "That feels good, no, that doesn't feel good," but listen to their actual bodies. You can tell. And you have to put that energy into it. To finding out what works. Try stuff out. There's a lot of other real estate besides the nipples and the vagina. A neck is a beautiful part of a woman; the ears, the belly. Be curious to see what turns her on. I swear to God, I would rather—and maybe this is just me at fifty-one—I'd rather have a woman have ten orgasms than me have ten orgasms.

Ali: Is that because you've been with so many women, you can afford to make that choice?

John: It turns me on more to see a woman get turned on, more than anything. Do the listening. I can tell, you can tell. And if you can't tell, talk about it out loud together.

Ali: Do you think, based on the amount and variety of women you've slept with, that it makes you a better lover?

John: You'd have to ask them. I hope I'm a decent lover.

Said so much like someone who probably is.

Ali: The first time you had sex, was it a nightmare, a mess? Are you actually like everybody else?

John: It was like, this is what the whole world revolves around? I didn't quite get it. You know I did that show [*Losing It with John Stamos*] about losing your virginity, so I've talked about this a lot. But it was an older woman who guided me through. But, as I got older and, I guess, becoming more of a caring person, I want someone to be turned on and I want to find out what turns her on. Maybe that comes from experience. Every woman is different. You can't ever do the exact same performance.

Ali: Is there one particular experience that stands out as your favorite?

John: Is the Mile High Club only with another person, or if you're in the bathroom by yourself, do you still get the wings? The real answer is, the times I've been most in love with someone, but who wants to read that? It's so boring.

Uhm, an entire swoony female population wants to read that. Though I'm also very certain he's got many more standout moments. I watch him as he's silent, scrolling through his own personal most-liked, but John here is uncharacteristically politic, perhaps polite. I wish he'd share, but kind of admire that he doesn't. But he does offer me something different. Something about him feeling . . . he doesn't use this word, he left it to the ellipses . . . but I think it's something like "used." Women having slept with him just to get a prize when they're done.

John: A few, a couple of women, have wanted to take "selfies" afterwards, when we're done, a picture of us together after the experience. One girl really wanted my shirt, like a souvenir.

Ali: Do you think many guys in your position would go, "Who cares why this woman wants to fuck me? I fucked her." So what if they want your shirt or a picture, is the experience lessened because they do?

John: Yes, of course it is. I mean, I had long-term relationships until my forties. I had girlfriends. I was with someone for ten years. I wasn't out fucking as much as everybody thinks I was.

Ali: I have to ask you your "number." How many women have you been with?

John: It's not as high as you might think. In my twenties and thirties, I had girlfriends and long-term relationships, and now I have morals.

Ali: Has a woman ever turned you down?

John: All the time. Sometimes my . . . fame . . . sort of works against me. Some women think, "Hey, just 'cause you're John Stamos, you don't automatically get to fuck me." So, in a sense, I cock-block myself. In

some ways, it takes me longer because I need to overcome their assumptions about me. They think I do this
all the time, so they feel less special, whether or not
that's true. Or conversely, I've gone out with women
and I don't do anything, and she complains afterwards
that she just wanted me to bend her over a table.

Ali: What was your worst sexual experience?

John: Well, it's not my worst, but I had an experience
where a girl I was dating for a month, we finally got to
the place when it was "the night." It was going to happen. And, I'm very self-conscious, I have to take, like,
fifteen showers, make sure my breath is great. And it's
happening and I'm going to give this woman oral sex
and I took, like, thirty minutes before I even got near
her vagina, and she was ready. And I knew this was
going to be a relationship, so I wanted it to be great.
So, I got to the arena and there's a very strange . . . there
was an unusual . . . a mass . . . something that wouldn't
ordinarily be there. It was a weird texture, a lump, but
it wasn't a medical thing. I kept licking it, checking at it
with my tongue and was like, what the fuck is this
thing? So it was me going, "Shit, I really care about this
person and I really want to continue this, but what the
fuck is this thing?" You know what it was? It was my
gum that I'd been chewing from before because I
wanted to make sure I had good breath. And we finished that part and she went to the bathroom and she
was like, "John. Why is there fucking gum in my pubic

hair?" (I was very impressed here that any woman John dated made the choice not to wax her pubic hair.)

Ali: Is there one piece of advice you'd hand out based on your personal experiences: how to get laid in just one sentence?

John: I can't give a guy advice who only wants to go get laid, 'cause I don't do that.

Ali: Okay, okay, let me reword it, see if I can sneak it past what a nice guy you are. Is there a piece of advice that will continuously connect someone to women? Not just a random person, but how to connect to a partner, a girlfriend or wife?

John: Well, sure. You have to think of them first. And if you do, ultimately, you're going to get what you want, anyway.

Ali: Do you think because you've had more experiences with women, it allows you to be more aware than most men?

John: I always want to make sure a woman gets everything she wants and more before I finish, because once, you know, once men ejaculate, it's kind of done. Like, "Where's the pizza, let's turn on the TV." So, I want to make sure she's good. But I guess that's from experience.

Ali: Because that's the man you are? Not because that's the famous man you are?

John: I want people to have that experience of me as giving, but not just women, and not just a woman I may sleep with. Sorry, that's not going to be interesting for your book.

Ali: My thesis isn't for you to seem like you're better because you've maybe had more, at all. It's just to get the perspective of someone who has probably had more than most.

John: If I have done more, that's not experience, that's patience. Good things take a while. You have to think about giving first. I don't just mean giving in sex, but giving, you know, in life.

And, by the way, yes, he paid for our breakfast, citing, "I have yogurt money."

Bottom line, if you really are terrifically handsome, please become really great at something else. Learn from Stamos. Every man should pick up drumming because it will teach you a consistent sense of rhythm and, even better, listening for the beat of the whole band. Playing drums will get you laid. Also, I learned that anyone with an exceptional handicap like fame or wealth, or an unusually thick or long penis, should take up a hobby. Focus on something/anything outside of yourself, even though life will discourage you from doing this. You must learn to listen to needs other than your own. In sex and in life, polish the thing that is less shiny about you, and you will get laid more, and better.

Chapter 8

How to Fuck a Woman

(Size does matter: an extra-long, girthy chapter)

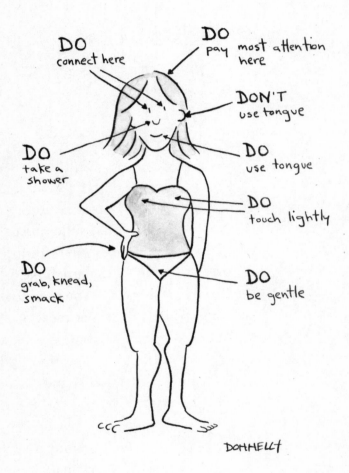

For those of you who thumbed or swiped directly to this chapter, congratulations. You do the exact same thing in sexual situations. In reading, just as in life, you cannot skip right to the best part and not expect to suffer the consequences of the shortcuts of ignorance. You're running around plucking out only the heart of the artichoke, but there are still all those thorny leaves to pull. You need to do some work in order to appreciate the proper meat of the matter. I mean, sure, you *can* skip stuff, but you're going to wind up doing a half-assed job. And this is a job you really want. Your inclination to skip to this final chapter is the exact same muscle you need to learn to curb in all things, not just in your fuck life.

Okay. Let's say you have a live, willing adult female who wants to have sex with you. This is optimal. So let's pretend you've never done this before. I know almost all of you have, but let's pretend you don't have a series of "moves"—habits you've accrued that we'll call your sexual repertoire. Let's not judge them, or what you've done in the past. Let's just wipe our slate clean right now. Pretend, for argument's sake, that you have no idea what you're doing. So, as with anything new, you must approach it with a requisite wide-eyed wonder. You wouldn't just jump head-first into hang gliding or diamond cutting or catching a bullet with your teeth. And remember, you're not going to be perfect the first day on the job. There is a practice to this business. The good news: practice is also fun.

The Vagina Golden Rule

I do not claim to know how to fuck every single woman. Each one is unique. There are no hard and fast rules, except to be willing to adapt to any given situation. Go with it. Pay close attention to what she says and does, as she generally provides all the hints you will ever need to complete this job successfully. But here is the most important Vagina Golden Rule. *Do not* do unto it as you would have done unto you. *Everything* about you is very different from a woman.

We must accept certain generalities about how to extract orgasms from the female gender. These are like the rules of poker. Then, we must wait and see the cards we are dealt, and apply these general rules to the individual. Each deal is unique. And each player brings her own history and habits, her "tells," or the psychology of how she plays her hand. Your job is to read someone's face (body, emotions, vagina) and glean how they're wired, and know when she's bluffing. Then we apply the general rules, knowing that these are the broad basics for successful interaction.

One of the most important things to remember is that while you get in the mood through physical connection, women also require a blast of emotional connection. That's what some of the previous chapters have covered: how to state your feelings and acknowledge hers as different from yours. All of that has brought you to this chapter for some practical information.

You must pay attention to all areas of your performance. After all, with texting and Facebook and apps like Lulu (where women actually review and rate men, like a Yelp guide to guys), the information about your sexual acumen isn't just some whispering about your reputation anymore. Women are making up for lost time and actually writing on the Internet bathroom wall. Everything, everywhere, all the time is now on your permanent record. So, please, try to do a good job.

Less Is More, Especially with Kissing

Now let's break it down.

For women, the moment before the first kiss is sometimes better than the actual first kiss. Play along like you think so, too. A kiss is the litmus test for fucking. If your kiss is gross, often things go no further than this. Get it right and set things up in your favor.

A kiss should most usually start soft—no tongue at first—and just like sex, *it should build in intensity*. You're the guy; most of the time, you take the lead. Be gentle, but strong, especially at first. Set the tone, but take cues from her. Don't go leaping in. Your tongue is not a Mars rover; it is not an exploration device programmed to bring saliva samples back to NASA. As Robert Browning wrote, "Less is more." Mies van der Rohe borrowed this as a concept for minimalist design. Minimalism is a good rule of tongue. Obviously use your tongue a little, but pay attention to the way she responds.

Almost every woman I know has endured a bad-kissing experience:

> "One guy kissed me like he was sticking his
>   tongue through a peephole."
> "One guy kept exhaling deeply into my mouth.
>   Sighs of relief, or resuscitation?"
> "One guy kept kissing me like he learned how
>   from watching the quiet, slick-haired men in
>   black and white movies."
> "One guy kissed me like he was a dental instru-
>   ment, checking each molar for plaque."

Kissing is as easy as anything else. Taking her cues and being in synch while acting like you know what you're doing. Carrying yourself with confidence.

Don't forget your hands, either. Use them, but not yet in an overtly sexual way. Make her feel safe; let her know that your hands are strong and in the exact right place they should be for a kiss. Her neck. Shoulders. Her waist. Maybe the small of her back, as you draw her in. The way in which she leans into you will give you more insight. Don't startle her by squeezing her tits. It will feel too invasive, too quickly. I know you want to squeeze them because a kiss says yes, and tits are the precursor to a vagina. Vagina, ergo, precursor to penis. If you get to penis, it's going to get you to that awesome release.

But calm the fuck down and pay attention to her cues. If she wants her tits squeezed (fondled sounds so Brontë sisters), she will continue to kiss you. She will probably put her hands around your neck, now allowing you free access. So put off the boob takedown for a few more seconds. Exhibit discipline. Count to yourself. Break your nature. Wait a little longer than you want to. Just a little. One Mississippi. Two Mississippi. Three Mississippi. So much of good fucking is delayed gratification and the glory of the buildup. So, okay, you'll move your hands to her breasts. If she responds well to this, stay there longer than you might want to before trying to crazily dash around the bases. The base system has fucked up many generations of overly anxious men. Four Mississippi.

The Tease Is Better Than the Squeeze

Regarding breasts: every woman is, of course, different. Look at all the diverse sizes and shapes of breasts out there. Of course they all feel different to their variety of owners. I would say, in general, breasts aren't as big a turn-on for us to have squeezed as for you guys to squeeze them. Mostly because we don't trust you. Sometimes too little or too much touch can be annoying. And you can't always know what we want in any given moment. So err on the side of caution, unless instructed otherwise. Nipples are extremely sensitive—or more rarely, not at all. Usually though, a giant overzealous tug can actually hurt, ripping a lady right out of the mood. And then instead of getting prepared to stick it in, you'll be like, "Oh, sorry, sorry . . ."

One must approach these delightful orbs gingerly, and adapt accordingly. A sound of pleasure emitting from their owner might encourage you to continue the kind of touch you're using. But, regardless of the noises she may be making, don't keep up a too constant, too strong grip. Stop as soon as she gets too used to something. The rule is soft, and then not-soft. Gentle to slightly rougher, never too rough—unless she passionately screams at you to do otherwise—that's the build. In all of this. The whole thing. From kiss to squeeze to finger to lick to fuck. It's all a give and take, and then loop back again. It's moving from gentle to a little more intense, and then back. Constant nipple stimulation can be extremely grating. We don't want to admonish you but we will retreat, sometimes just in our heads, by disengaging and disconnecting if it's too annoying.

We are the same as you in this area. We are the same as you are in every other interactive dynamic. We will tune you out to get it done. We love sex when it's performed properly. But if it's not done the way we like it, sometimes rather than correct you in the middle of it and risk hurting your fragile ego, some women may grin and bear it (see:

faking orgasms) just to get through it. It's women's version of men listening to our overly detailed, often irrelevant stories about our incredulity over some guy at work whose kidneys continue to function despite the fact that he drinks forty cups of coffee every day.

How many men have ever faked an orgasm if a woman is lousy at sex? In general, you don't care if a female is bad at sex as long as you're having sex. Either way, odds are, even if she's total crap at it, you will come.

So, if you want to keep us in the game, don't fixate on the boobs because you'll distract or annoy us to the point of quitting. Don't go squeezing everything all the time. Some women like it rougher, but even then, it's often the *absence* of what a woman wants that arouses her the most.

Rhyming rule of thumb: the tease is often better than the squeeze. And, oh please, I know it's tempting, but don't suck too much or too hard on the nipples. They're very sensitive, but it also makes her think your mom didn't nurse you properly, which grosses her out. Neither does she want a million tiny tongue circles around and around in annoying Apolo Ohno speed-skating repetition. Everything in sex is catch and release. It's both repetition and switching it up. Until it's not.

Deciphering the Confusing Parts

In order to fuck a woman, you have to understand what it is you're dealing with down there. And no lady wants to lie back on the bed with her legs open and the lights on. She doesn't want to take out a laser pointer and indicate which parts of her require the most, or gentlest attention. There are lots of confusing parts to deal with, I know. It's over-whelming. It's practically an astronomical constellation: labias minora and majora. It's why men generally prefer less pubic hair. It's one more mystery removed; one less layer to decipher. Maybe they can try to piece together what the hell is going on down there if it's bald. I know that the totality of the vagina scares you. It scares us *for* you. Pro-vided you can get it up, your genitals are fairly simple. Something provides friction and presto, blasto. But our private parts are like complicated motherboards. You need a loupe and gloves just to check out what the fuck you're working with down there.

Now I'm sure women will yell at me here when I say what a complicated-looking thing a vagina is upon initial presentation. The expression upon first seeing it must be the face people make when they travel to Paris, order the exotic-sounding *escargot*, and are stunned to receive a plate of snails. Sure, after eating the butter and garlic–drenched mollusks, most agree they're delicious. But what a stunning first impression. A vagina must be quite the curiosity to have to decipher upon first introduction. This is why I'm here to help.

Let's part the constellations, labias majora and minora, and discuss the two most important areas: the location of the clitoris, and the actual part of the vagina that has always interested you. From Boardwalk to Park Place, the most expensive and fantastic real estate that exists in the canal, the length between the vulva and the cervix.

The Most Sensitive Spot in the World

Now, some men refer to the clitoris as the Little Man in the Boat. This seems odd, as it implies that a man always sits in the same northern seat in a boat, and an ignorant man might take a southern seat closer to the anus if he didn't know any better. Also, "clitoris" sounds like something added to toothpaste to keep your teeth extra white. But let's please stop referring to it as "the little man in the boat" or a woman's "tiny penis" or a "pleasure button." Let's simply refer to it as the key relevant area near the vagina that will get your woman off.

How can I write a book about fucking a woman without using *the* word? You know the one with the uncatchy nickname: clit. Testicles have so many adorably catchy nicknames . . . balls, nuts, sac, all so much more squirrel related and animated than they actually are. But "clit" is harsh sounding. Maybe you don't want to *say* it aloud, but please don't forget about it.

Let's assume the statistic is true that 80 percent of all women cannot achieve an orgasm through intercourse alone. The rare sighting of the Loch Ness vaginal orgasm only occurs in about 20 percent of women. The most sensitive spot on her needs direct, or even better, *indirect but adjacent stimulation,* until fruition. She doesn't have a wide expanse of super-sensitive skin for her genitals the way you

Ali Adler

do; instead, she has this one tiny but powerful cluster. Of course penetration feels good and amazing, but for her to actually come, most likely you will need to perform a secondary motion that rouses her clit.

If she comes while you are inside her, without your stimulating her clitoris directly with your hand, then your body (probably your abdomen) is somehow pushing consistently against her clitoris. The continuous motion of your thrusting may make her come. But any way you slice it, it is almost always some stimulation of her clitoris that will finish her off.

Besides how she feels about her weight, her clit is the most sensitive area on a woman's body. As little girls, we were all taught not to kick our brothers in the balls because their testicles were so super-sensitive. Whatever is inside testes will cure cancer, so don't jostle them in any way. The fate of the world relies on these things. But a woman's clitoris is even more sensitive. In fact, direct pressure will make her squirm away and in the worst-case scenario, shoo you out of the bedroom. But if you've located this zone and can find the opposite of your instinctual touch, you'll cause much pleasure for this woman.

Eight Thousand Nerve Endings Deserve Special Treatment

Despite what you may think, the clitoris is nothing at all like a tiny penis. Please don't think it is, even if, biologically, it originated from the same bundle of tissue in utero. Generally speaking, it doesn't want hard friction. There are many variations in how different women like to be touched here. Sure, some like to be mashed with chronic pressure, and constantly stimulated. But these women are in the minority. These types of clitorises, and the woman attached to them, are luckier for you because this is more how you touch yourself. But the more common clitoral proprietor is the woman who enjoys only a smidge of pressure, then less pressure, then more pressure, then less pressure, then consistent pressure (albeit lighter than you may imagine)—and then she'll come.

So, just as in life, you must treat her clitoris the opposite of what your instincts encourage you to do. You think, "Oh, if this is a woman's most sensitive area (like your own jolly penis), then I'll give it the same friction and strength that I like." Uhm, no, stop that. Your penis is a hunk of skin, and the whole thing is quite sensitive. But, in general, the bulk of our pleasure emanates from this one tiny zone, so it has far more nerve endings. Allegedly eight thousand nerve endings, which is four times the amount as on the head of your dick. It's the fucking epicenter and the epicenter of fucking, so please, be respectful. Be gentle.

When you touch this precious gem, make sure your hands are clean and fingernails trimmed. Take your hands and approach it with the same tenderness as if you were to delicately lift a ladybug off an octogenarian nun's habit, or pick a tiny eyelash off your six-year-old daughter's face in order for her to still be able to qualify for a decent wish. Please don't take a run at that thing. You don't want to squash it. You sidle up next to it and, like a magnet and iron, allow it to lean towards you. It's a bull's-eye, but the area around it is also very sensitive, so those points count, too.

If you are near it but not on it, the woman will bend herself into you, allowing a passive touch that, if you are paying attention, is instructive and will allow you to continue purposefully and with confidence. Yes, the clitoris is so smart that if you're touching it properly, it will actually encourage you. If you are listening well, it will almost always tell you what to do. It's the brain of the operation. If you are gently moving it, your woman will make pleasureable noises. These noise emissions are trying to guide you and encourage you to continue doing what you are doing.

Touching a woman there is a little like very tiny cross-country skiing. You don't mash the snow down. You move your feet gently back and forth, gliding across the top of the snow, trying to get to your destination. Pretend your finger is one ski and the tip is touching the snow. Your finger is the elliptical machine of the clitoris. But keep in mind the aforementioned bull's-eye wisdom; you don't always need to hit the nail right on the head. Sometimes the best area of the epicenter is slightly off to one side or the other (still on it, just not directly on it, we collectively beg you). If you listen carefully to her breathing, you should know if she's a middle of the road, a lefty, or a righty. And if you blindly do your elliptical movements directly atop the belly of the beast, it can take her off track and there she is again, back at square one. It's a woman's version of the pinball machine's tilt button. You will be exhausted and impatient and she will be annoyed, and no one will have won.

Basics about Fucking That Every Man Should Know

A few basic things to know about fucking a woman.

Women are extremely aware of their bodies. Most of them live in their heads. They spend so much time in there, having imaginary conversations with you. They need permission to exit. You can help them with this by connecting emotionally, as we've discussed earlier, but another huge hurdle to overcome is to help women push past their own innate inhibitions. You may ask, "God, when does it stop with these people? When is enough, enough?" I know, I get it. Sorry. I don't know what to tell you. If women are too complicated for you, go fuck a man. Attracted to their genitals or not, they are way simpler. The dick gets hard, it needs release. If you want a woman—and I do, too—it just *is* this complex. In general, the less complicated of us are less interesting. Some do exist, but they are usually your mothers, so that won't work out, either.

So much of sex for women is mental. Sometimes women's body insecurities or inhibitions won't allow them to relax. Here is where you come in. When you get down there, your face right up on her, as an overall tonal note, you must behave as if her vagina is the greatest thing you've ever smelled, tasted, and had the privilege to be near. She must believe that she is letting you eat the Cinnabon that is attached to her body.

No matter how you really feel about it or how intimidated you are, she needs to believe you've never been near such a source of sweet light. Her vagina, and all your senses that have the privilege of being near it, are meeting the pope. (Yes, pussy and pope were just in side-by-side sentences.) Her vagina is the fountain of youth. It's true; all roads have led up to this delectable moment. Make believe that it is the apex of all positive things that have ever happened to you in life. And maybe it is. But if you demonstrate that this is your attitude about it, she will take a page from your behavior and *feel* like it, too. Even if you're not that good at going down on a woman yet, you will make her feel so relaxed in this moment that she will help you by being very open with communication, verbal and nonverbal. The clues that she emits are invaluable.

Truth is, love it or not, you have to eat it like you love it. Like the Sugarhill Gang sings, it's like going over to your friend's house to eat when you were a kid; you don't know what the fuck his parents are going to serve you. Maybe it's nothing you've ever eaten before, nothing that looks or tastes like what your family has ever prepared for dinner— but, to make everyone feel good, you're going to have to clean that plate. You must eat that gloppy gravy-riddled pork chop as if it's the most delicious thing you've ever tasted, the best dish you've ever been served. You love it. You ask for seconds before finishing your firsts. You sop up the sauce with your bread, savoring each bite. You ask your friend's mom how she made it; you want to give your own mother the recipe. This analogy is getting slightly too Oedipal, but you get my point. If you clean your plate like you've never tasted anything more delicious, you're going to get asked back for dinner another night. Love it, sniff it like it's a very expensive bottle of wine, be into it, and delight in it. Make her feel like she's the best wine you've ever swallowed. Twenty bucks a sip.

Yes, it is a physiological game, but you will put the woman so at ease with your being down there that whatever you choose to do, right or less right, she will go with it. You do get points for enthusiasm here. Make her feel like if she were to take away your right to eat her pussy, you'd be devastated. A kid unable to eat the Tootsie Roll center of the Tootsie Pop. If she is shy, fight for your right to eat her. Demand it. Say it's selfish, that it turns you on, that you want to do it not for her, but for you. She will get so into it that it may actually become your favorite dish.

Practice on a Peach

You don't need to have an actual vagina available to practice this, although it sure does help. But, if necessary, you can practice on your own time, too. Take a tip from T. S. Eliot and go out and dare to eat a ripe peach. If you don't like peaches, I don't give a shit; pretend that you like peaches. Ripe peaches are juicy and messy. They are not neat to eat. Softly press your lips up against it, like you're going to whisper something super sexy to this piece of fruit. Move your lips on it gently, feel the light fuzz of the peach touching and tickling your lips. File away this memory. It seems so insignificant and small, but this level of sensitivity training is everything. This is vaginal boot camp. Do tongue push-ups until it hurts.

Bookmark your awareness, because you're going to need it later when you get rid of this dummy stone fruit and replace it with the real thing. Drag your tongue across it. In real life, you will be doing this to figure out what's what and part her down the middle. You can also just part her area very gently with your hands. As if clasping your hands in prayer, which couldn't hurt, open up all the lips that totally fucking confuse you. You won't fuck this up if you stay away from the sensitive tippy-top, initially. Smell her with joy, as if she is some sort of delicious baked good, warm and fresh from the oven. You can't wait to gobble this down. Then, lick it a little, using the tip of your tongue at first to get your bearings, metaphorically sipping it and then, tongue flatter, lap it gently up and down now as if you are a cat who spilled your damn saucer of milk in there. I know you think you're eating her pussy now, licking it like this, and you are, but this is still the *amuse-bouche*, as it were.

Most of this is really just priming her pump. Make sure it's as good and goddamned juicy as all those peaches you spent your summer checking for bruises and practicing on. If you lick this thing with the flat middle of your tongue, at the top of her, there is a very responsive area that won't flatten or mash down with your lick. This is the super-sensitive clit, and as I've mentioned, it is an area of gentle caution but also of potentially fantastic glory. Now, I'm asking you not to be intimidated by this thing, but do not yet touch it directly with your tongue. Instead, purse your lips LOOSELY around the whole area as if it is a nuclear warhead/tip of a straw. Create a light vacuum suction around it with the same lip sensitivity, as you were able to ascertain the light fuzz of the peach. Now go gently back and forth with little slow kitten licks inside of your mouth vacuum. Get her into a relaxed rhythm of your being here. Faster, slower, but the same pressure. A consistent motoring of your tongue. Let her trust your mouth.

This can go on for a while. And then, whoa. Just stop. Don't move out of position even a centimeter (I only hand out cunnilingus tips in metric). Just stop your tongue. Lightly break the vacuum seal. Wait, what? She will be irked; she was just getting into it. If she is in the proper head-space from your head, she will grind into you to encourage you/compliment what you were doing. Now you will have a fair gauge of how much she liked it, and you are also using the catch-and-release method described earlier. Here and gone. Tame her, and then make her feel your absence, if only for what feels for her like a terribly long second. She will think this is cruel, a good/mean tease, especially as her rhythm intensifies. But she'll also respect you for knowing the cues of her body. It's the same rule as all the rest of these chapters: "know me." Don't do this trick too many times, as it can seriously throw everything off and ruin all your hard (but fun) work. Try it out a couple of times. She may respond by reaching down and mashing your face further down into her, which is a great sign that things are going very well.

Using Your Fingers and Hands

Going down on a woman requires a certain one-man-band quality of lovemaking that can be physically arduous. But, ultimately, it's an investment in yourself, so learn to do more than just use your tongue while you're down there. A guy I worked with once told me the reason he never went out dancing with his wife was although he understood intuitively how his body should move to the beat, he admitted, "I don't know where to put my hands." And I don't either when I'm dancing. But I know where to put them when going down on a lady.

Make solid use of the excellent tools attached to your body, these hands of yours. They can be underneath her, squeezing and happily grabbing two ass cakes. Or they can be holding her thighs apart or even pushing her legs apart for your easier and eventual access. But it's also fair to say that a snack, let's call them finger foods, won't spoil her dinner. Fingers take nothing away from what you will soon provide for her with your dick. However, to my recollection, your dick can't bend and contort the way a finger can inside a woman. Teasing her with your finger or fingers is like a very gripping trailer, a coming attraction to the main feature that you and your penis will soon be playing.

A side note on fingering: you may wonder, "What's in it for me? How does fingering her help me out at all?" Think about your car's dipstick. How it is an empirical reading of what's going on inside your car's oil thingama-jig. This gives you a fair test of your woman's natural viscos-ity levels. Simply, wetness is confirmation that she's into it. It will illustrate to you very clearly that if your levels are low, add some oil. Use your finger as a dipstick; obviously your tongue won't work.

Which brings me to your tongue. If your dipstick does show low internal moisture, you're not done with foreplay. Don't be confused here. Her vagina seems wet. Of course it is; you were just slobbering all over it. Make sure this wet-ness is *her* wetness, and not your saliva. So get out that dipstick finger and check your lady's internal moisture lev-els. If she isn't wet enough and she's telling you she's into it, that she's all ready, she's a liar. You simply haven't done enough to get her going, or she's just not into you. The vagina never tells lies, that sweet thing.

A sort of science test: touch your thumb and forefinger together. If there's a slight stickiness, congratulations, you've struck oil! I know, this seems like a terrific time for you to put your penis inside her now that the traffic light appears to be very green-for-go, but just like before, hang on. One Mississippi. Two Mississippi. Three Mississippi. As you resume your light vacuum seal on her clit while simul-taneously licking and sucking lightly, stick one finger (you can always add more; they aren't very far away and cost absolutely zero to access) inside her as you lick. You can use the middle finger, the traditional "fuck" finger and/or its Sir Lancelot finger standing by, the index finger. Or maybe your personal preference is the "fuck" finger plus the ring finger that can also act in concert as a helper friend.

Prior to putting this or these fingers up inside her, please take the time to notice: your digits are divided into three sections. Technically they are the distal phalanx, the middle phalanx, and the proximal phalanx. You can examine their bends during your summer peach-eating sessions. Now, look—if you turn your fingers towards you, there is a natural curl to them; they don't only shoot out straight. Practice this "c'mere" gesture using these fingers. Now, as they enter your woman, gently at first, use this same "c'mere" action. In fact, this finger or fingers, while inserted straight, should now be bending backwards into the letter C if they are hitting the area they are supposed to. They are on a very specific quest right now. They crook backwards towards the attic of the vagina. For orientation purposes, the tips of them should be pointing back at you. "Wait. What . . . why?" you may ask. "Why wouldn't they just go straight on up into her (emulating your cock)?" Because right now you're attempting to find the elusive G-spot. This is where it lives, up in this secret annex.

Still in this same "c'mere" position, tap-tap-tap your fingers on the attic of her vagina with your fingers in this button-hooked formation. One clue that you'll know you've finger-stumbled into it is that the skin where you're tapping is slightly rougher to the touch. Another, larger clue should be her quickened breathing and sudden agreement, "Yes! Yes!" Her new manners, "Please! Please!" Or her interest in religion, "Oh God! Oh God!" With a degree of practice, you can even continue to pleasure her with your tongue while tap-tap-tapping on this often-forgotten-about area. Listen to her breathing as she starts to come. Between all the licking and the tapping, stay consistent with your movements. Hallelujah!

How to Know When to Stick It In

After she finishes coming, your dick is now on deck. But, just when you think she's finished, pause for a few seconds and then maybe even start the whole oom-pah-pah band up again. Some women can come multiple times. The point is, finish her off good, as many times as possible, and that number may just be one. Many women don't orgasm multiple times. Some do. Don't push it if she seems happy. But when she is done, go ahead and fuck her. Try to take your time, but don't worry about it; she's satisfied. You have wholeheartedly earned this now. See? Doesn't it feel better to have worked so hard plucking out all those pesky, pointy artichoke leaves, and not just quickly gobbling down the heart?

Of course when you get good at all of this, you can switch it up. So much of sex is knowing the person you're doing it with and what she enjoys and responds to. Once you familiarize yourself with your partner's likes and how her unique body responds and operates, you can manually stimulate her while you simultaneously fuck her. If you can master this, you've got a shot at the really big win: coming at the same time. But don't get too caught up in that. If you can't come together, just prioritize her orgasm. We all know you'll come. Just make her come before you do. Then you can check it off your list and be totally selfish. Or another option is fuck her then pull out before you finish up. Focus only on making her come so she mistakes you for a man who cares. Then, afterwards, do whatever the hell you want; come in ten quick and easy strokes. You're cool with her.

An overall tonal tip; one that is true in all pieces of fucking and/or seducing a woman emotionally or otherwise. It is conquer and retreat.

Sure, you should fuck her, but the absence of fucking her leaves her in a state of wanting, which is almost as pleasurable. The longing and loss are physiologically/psychologically just as important as all the ramming and coming. It can't just be ram-ram-ram-pound-pound-pound, although I'm sure that's fun, too, but it's also the art of the tease. Don't just jam it on up there—go gradually so even those of you with less down there can feel like a much bigger deal when you're eventually using all of what you've got.

The Erogenous Zones of a Female (the dos and please do-nots)

The Brain. DO. I know this is a very annoying answer, but it's also very, very true. Head space is such a key area of sexual connectivity with women. Use your mouth. Yes, yes, sure cunnilingus, absolutely. But so much of who a woman is sexually is about how she's feeling inside her brain. It is extremely unusual to find a woman who, say, looks at a photo of a stranger's dick and scratches one out. (Your version of random porn, which we know excites you.) We are a less visceral bunch than you, in general.

Broadly speaking, a woman is aroused by her connectivity with you, although she may have internal distractions. Do your best to clear her mindfield and command her attention. A woman needs mental stimulation as much as you need the opposite. So use your mouth this way, too: talk dirty. Set the stage. Force her to pay attention to what's actually happening right now in the moment. Allay her insecurities. Put her in a different head space than where she is now. She may be worrying about her day at work tomorrow, or if your thirsty four-year-old will wander into your room just as you finally get Mommy up on all fours. "Oooo, uhhhh, Daddy and I are playing choo-choo. Yes. Daddy *does* get to be the caboose."

Maybe she is distracted; wondering when was the last time she showered or if she's too bloated from the big meal you just ate, or if her period is really finished up yet. These things matter to her. I know, you don't care about any of that stuff when *you're* all worked up. (YOU are a human male animal engaged in a primal mating ritual. This is supposed to be a dirty business, and you fucking love it!) But she does get caught up in her brain, so it's up to you to distract her from her internal concerns and inhibitions. Dominate her mentally. Command her attention. If she's too quiet, it means she's drifting off into a haze of fears, daily internal nagging, or insecurities. Make it so there's no wiggle room for her to go back to her work to-dos or thinking about where she may have stored your child's inoculation card. I know this seems impossible, because for you, sex is so in-the-moment and tactile, but women have a very distractible mental component as well.

The Nose. DO. Forget about cologne; I'm talking about pheromones. The natural chemistry your body emits. This shit is real. Smell means a lot. Some people are just naturally more attracted to each other scentwise. And I don't mean hygiene. By this point, I expect that you are groomed and ready for lady action. I mean, what you smell like when you sweat can be a very sexy thing for a specific woman. What your natural emissions are—yes, including *those* emissions—some woman may love, while someone else may not be into how you smell and taste at all. And you're not doing anything differently. You're not showering more or drinking an ungodly amount of mythically semen taste–improving pineapple juice or eating lawns of parsley. You are just you. Some people just have a greater "scent match" than others. Sometimes you just do all that licking business down there because you *should*, but when you meet your "scent match," you'll do it because you have to; because you love it.

The eyes. DO. Sure, you want everything to look good, but she may like it if you take away this sense sometimes, too. The absence of sight provides you with the ability to switch things up on her, keep her guessing as to what move you'll make. The deprivation of any of her senses is always erotic, if she's into this. Don't kiss her on the eyes though, or she won't take you seriously ever again.

The mouth. DO. Kiss it, sure, but you can also speak words to your sexual advantage. Dirty talk. Think of it as aural sex.

Ears. NO!!! DO NOT. This one tops the list of awful things done in bed that men think women love. Get your tongues out of our ears. Put them inside the vaginas, please. Or lick up dead flies along the windowsill if you simply *must* use your tongue in that moment, but just please keep them out of the insides of our ears. The ear lick is wet and echoey, and not at all pleasant for you or anyone else. It is a tongue Q-Tip that resounds and leaves behind a wet glob that we can't even politely sop up without fear of offending you and your creative but repellant ear-licking. Also, it's confusing. It breaks the cardinal rule of "Men do to you what they want done to them." If we can have accomplished one thing here, just stop with the inside of the ears business.

The vagina. DO. Obviously, yes. Please do. Read above advice. I literally can't type the word "clitoris" one more time without risking that it will be the Andy Cohen drinking game Word of the Day on *Watch What Happens Live*. Clit. Clit. Clit. Drunk, yet? Clitoris.

The breasts. DO. See above treatise on bosoms, large and small.

The ass. DO. This thing needs stronger stimulation than breasts, because it has fewer nerve endings. Don't be as gingerly as you were warned to be with the tits. Try a little ass grab; knead it, pat it, and smack it. However, please leave the rectum alone unless previously discussed or instructed.

Rules to Remember

- So much of sexual congress is just that: being in agreement. Be into it. Be into her. Forget about yourself for fifteen fucking minutes in your entire life. Pay attention to sinking into this person more than just literally.
- It's as much the art of pressure and friction as it is the absence of friction.
- It's as much the art of consistency as it is about inconsistency.
- Stop asking stupid questions like, "Why isn't the clit inside, at the end of the vagina so that the penis can rhythmically stroke it?" I understand your design point, but it's not. Stop playing like it is.
- Just sticking your dick in and moving it around and crossing your fingers and hoping for the best for her orgasm will not work.
- Unless you're in your twenties or in the first two months of your relationship or on MDMA or Molly or Ecstasy (U4EA!) or whatever the kids are calling it these days, don't worry about doing a 69. Just leave it in the past.

- Stop masturbating so much to Internet porn. It can get addictive. Cut it down. Come on, just a little. If you do it too often, it creates unrealistic expectations and desensitizes actual human-to-human physical encounters.
- Ninety percent of the women I surveyed in relationships are the instigators of sexual activity with their male partners. A staggering statistic. Men want it all the time, but they've learned that if they try to instigate it, they may be rejected. So a Darwinian reflex occurs where the women must be the instigator. Pretend you're not into it, and see how much more ass you obtain. Women want what they can't have.
- It's okay to mix stuff up, but ultimately—in sex, as in relationships—women want reliable.

How to Spice Up Sex with the Same Vagina

The long-term relationship. Sigh. When we commit to have sex with just the one person over and over again until we're dead, it can become a little monotonous. So, how do you trick yourself into believing the same vagina is a fresh new one or, conversely, that the familiar one is even *better than* a new one? I don't think any man will totally be okay knowing that other men are out there conquering brand new vaginas while he's back at home nursing his familiar one. Something about hunters and warriors, the conquest of the unknown and all that. But if you have made this oath to be faithful to the same one, here's some stuff you can do to stay connected sexually so you can stay connected emotionally, which is the ultimate conquest.

- Remember when? Do it how you did it when you first started doing it. Remember those BJs she used to give you while you were driving? I know you're somebody's dad now, but you love BJs the exact same amount now as you did back then. You used to fuck on the beach . . . do that again. You used to make out. Get back to that. Delete the phrase "Remember when we used to . . ." Instead, resume doing it.
- Switch up roles. If you lead more often, encourage her to take charge more. Get out of your time-worn habits. You know, your sexual go-to. The usual. Lick it and stick it. Whatever your standard thing is, shake it up. Do the opposite of what the usual is, and suddenly your usual will become the unusual. Ugh, I know you can barely stomach the thought, but take a bath with her. Wash her back. Pretend it doesn't have some acne on it. Get into bed without the expectation of sex now that your balls are clean. She'll be so startled and feel so little pressure that she will initiate it herself.

- Share your fantasies/role play. Say the stuff you're scared to say aloud to your wife. Scary. She actually knows you, so now she'll really know you. Scroll past the ones you know she knows about—threesomes, anal, exhibitionism—and get to something really vulnerable about yourself. "I always think about a certain nun from high school forcing me to have sex with her." Huh? Well, she's got to step aside from judgment. Because no matter how odd it is, it is true for you. And, she married you. She's certainly got to give it a whirl, even if she doesn't go out and buy a habit. It's when you don't risk saying what it is you secretly want that bitterness may accrue. Wait, what? You have resentment over her not understanding something you've never even shared aloud? That doesn't make a lot of sense, does it? Say what it is you want; you risk actually getting it.
- Schedule date night, but even less trite, schedule fuck time. Sure, everyone wants to eat a pizza and see a movie, but that advice is really about reminding ourselves to be intimate with the person we've chosen. So even if you have an obligatory Tuesday night date to fuck, the act of doing it actually allows it to happen much more frequently, and with a greater connection. Fuck, and you will fuck more. Also,

don't forget that you have a tendency to communicate less and be more emotionally distant if you have a bunch of unreleased sperm
in your nutsack. Release the sperm for a better
mood, ergo a higher rate of connection.

- Keep your damned kids out of your bed at
  night. It will create a far more fuck-friendly
  zone. Use the lock on your door. You can
  unlock it after you come, in case little Harper
  has a bad dream.

- Just do her sometimes. I get it: you need the
  release; but just show up somewhere and
  deliver her an orgasm. Then you may get back
  to work or kids or masturbating or whatever
  the hell you were doing before you put her
  needs ahead of your own.

- Add something new to your repertoire, whatever this may be for you. Maybe it's a new
  position. Maybe it's a new piece of lingerie or
  a sex toy. We all know science: that if you
  leave whatever is in the petri dish alone without any air or a new ingredient, the matter
  will die. So switch it up, add, subtract, reverse,
  but keep the dish alive at all costs.

A bonus piece of advice for women: stop faking orgasms.
How are men ever going to learn how to do it if you falsely
reward them?

Remember way back in the beginning, when I said men and women were different? Well, no shit. You already knew that. Now you're armed with some ideas as to how to minimize and embrace those differences. Nothing has really changed for you, except a new awareness of how deep this shit goes. And awareness is the first step to change. And look, I get it. Because I'm me, plus I'm with a woman, I know you'll keep trying to do it all your own way. And you get that I'm not even talking about fucking now, right? You just think your ways in general are correct. You know your partner is doing it wrong, but if only she would do it your way, life would be so much easier, and you two would be totally happy. So you'll continue doing life and fucking your same old way, maybe just now and then remembering to touch her clit a little bit more lightly.

Chapter 9

Breaking Up
Getting Rid of the Woman You've Got

"I hope that guy sees the warning signs."

You wanted her for so long, lusted after her for forever, before you fucked her. You even fucked your own fist, imagining it was her—but now you've actually had her over and over again. So many times, in fact, that now you imagine her vagina as your own fist. Thud. What the hell are you going to do now that she bugs the shit out of you?

The tonic of wanting her has worn off. Now she's actually yours. And who cares why. If you've gotten to this place, there's almost no turning the ship around. She calls you her boyfriend. You've met all the people in her life, even her parents, multiple tedious times. You look at her mother, with her weighty face and light wrinkles; the Pillsbury dough woman suit of plumped-in-the-oven menopause and the exhausted bags under her eyes. You project your own future as you assume that your girlfriend will age similarly. Her mother looks like things stopped pleasing her in the eighties. That the last time she had a good belly laugh or a dick in her mouth was the same night she watched *Mrs. Doubtfire* at the local theater.

Your girlfriend's father is everything that bugs you about your own gender. He has taken on the gratingly emasculated attitude of "happy wife, happy life." He's channeled all his previous fuck passion into a condescendingly excessive knowledge of decanting wine and toe-weighted putters. They squabble about passionless things: whose turn it is to pick what to watch on network television, brands of baked chips, and—said with a what-am-I-going-to-do-with-her smirk—can she ever learn to please stop letting the water run while she is brushing her teeth?

You observe their dynamics, and can't help but think about your own future. You see your projected future self wither; want to eat its own foot off in order to escape from the trap. You imagine your future semen only able to ejaculate in powdery puffs. You see a composite of your girlfriend's parents as the two people responsible for producing a woman who now has a rental agreement with your balls, and is looking to buy. But you want to break the lease and move on. So how do you do it when you've sworn you love the place?

Relax. Now you need to know how to break up with a woman.

In terms of commitment, some men are haunted by doubt, indecision, and what-ifs. You think, "What if I'm not sure I like the woman, once I'm in too deep?" "Is it possible to take back an 'I love you'?" "Is there such a thing as the word 'abortion'?" "How do I say no, forever, to the rest of the vaginas out there?" "What if I feel trapped, dead, and drowning?" "What if I always imagine there's something better out there, even when I'm relatively happy?" "How do I stop wanting warm, new pussy?" Or the most haunting that will ultimately shortchange you even more than her: "Is she the best I can do?" This chapter is about how to release a vagina after you've gone to such lengths to acquire it.

The Passive Breakup

One of the most cowardly ways to break up with a woman, but still a favorite, is the classic: the passive breakup. You basically become an emotionally withholding asshole until she gathers up enough sense of self and dumps you. That way, you can maintain your theoretical nice-guy status. Because you didn't do the actual breaking up. You didn't say the words "I want to end this." This method is a true measure of your girlfriend's self-esteem. Sometimes ignoring your passive-aggressive nonsignals and just blindly trying to fix something is her way of trying to remedy her own broken history.

You once adored this person above all else. You picked her and chose her and French kissed the contents of her underpants. So, please, remember that you once loved her, and don't use this method. Because here's how it goes: you are slowly and cruelly starving her to death by withholding all necessary life essentials, while not admitting that you're doing this. You think you're not being an asshole, but she's running around to all her best friends talking about you now more than ever. Asking them, polling them, wondering why you're so limited, why you're incapable of giving more, being less self-centered. They are preaching to her, sermonizing about valuing herself, about getting rid of you. They're telling her that she deserves more and better, and she fucking does.

But this is one of those times where you think it's much easier this way. You don't have to accept responsibility for anything, including your own inability to disconnect. This way, there's no heartbreaking confrontation. I know you really think it's better this way; that she's eventually going to draw her own conclusion and learn to value herself. But, in the meantime, you are scorching the earth. This method is even worse than the evil cheat-your-way-out method that seems self-explanatory enough not to have to get into. However, once your girlfriend's self-esteem is at an all-time low, she will cobble together the courage from her self-help books and jury of friends to break up with you. Eventually she will become the hero of the story; while you are, at best, the asshole and/or, at worst, a weak little pussy. She gets to be the one who bravely put a bullet in the relationship, ending your collective. She finally says some version of "This isn't working." "I can't do this by myself anymore." "I am less scared of the unknown than I am of (you) the known." "I thought there was something wrong with me, but now I know the thing wrong is you." Or the most culpable: "For a long time I blamed you, but now I blame myself for not creating what I deserve."

And as soon as she makes this sort of strength-exhib-iting declaration, all of a sudden she is power personified, has a sexy backbone, a sense of self. Now, as she radiates these fantastic qualities she had to gather together, all of a sudden, because of her excellence in this moment—*you want her again*. Oh, yeah, *this* one, *this* strong woman is the one you fell in love with originally. You're an ass.

Know this: throughout the time that you were starving her of love, you were also starving yourself. It's a lose-lose. So much for your not wanting to be the bad guy.

The Drama of the Diamond

I've seen this go very deep before.

A grown man with a child's nickname is always cause for trepidation. Years ago, I was in a writers' room with an adult man nicknamed something akin to "Cubby." At that time, people in the room were always making some major announcement or another. Seemed like every week there was a new milestone: someone getting engaged or announc-ing a pregnancy, having a wedding or a baby. We were all in such a state of blooming news. Anyway, Cubby, who had been in a relationship for about three years, would always avoid talking about it because engagements were popping up all around him. He felt a sidelong pressure from his girlfriend—let's call her Beth—and also from his peers and his parents, who adored her. Everyone liked Beth; Beth was amazing, Beth was elegant. The only nagging doubt about Beth was a universal feeling that maybe she was too normal for Cubby. Like, what was wrong with Beth that she even wanted to be with Cubby? Everyone agreed she was way too good for him.

So the whole room was very surprised when we came back from Christmas break to learn that Cubby was engaged. "What? To whom?" I kinda wondered. We were thrilled, wanted to hug and congratulate him, but he confessed it with the same *whatever* attitude as if he'd finally settled on what kind of new car to get. It wasn't the car of his dreams, but it got him to destinations reliably, got good gas mileage. Cubby did like to tell the story of spending a little too much money on a ring, and the whole drama around the retelling of his engagement anecdote. The drama of the diamond, of the last-minute FedExing of the ring to her parents' winter wilderness.

But I didn't really get his emotional shift. I wondered, "Why now?" What changed for him between when we left for winter break (the 23rd) and December 25? Turns out, Cubby had been wracking his brain, trying to come up with a decent present for Beth. Poor Cubby just couldn't think of anything else to get her for Christmas. They were going to be in Vermont, at her parents' white-columned home. So Cubby, knowing he was going to be a hero for presenting a piece of ice in front of her fancy parents, stopped considering getting her a new laptop and decided to propose.

So, Christmas morning, before the house started reeking of nutmeg, Cubby suggested they go outside for a walk before anyone else was awake. Beth knew Cubby hated exercise only as much as he hated chilly temperatures and itchy wool hats, but she went with it. He walked her outside behind her childhood home, got down on one of his creaky knees on the potentially creaky frozen lake and proposed marriage forever.

They came back into the warm house, and Cubby was clapped on the back by her father, a former college football player already slurping greasy eggnog at seven-thirty in the morning. For Cubby, getting engaged to the linebacker's daughter was like finally being accepted into the fraternity that wouldn't take him. His proposal usurped the holiday usually reserved for celebrating the birth of Jesus in this particular house. Cubby had gone out and spent thousands of dollars on a ring, knowing he didn't really want to marry Beth. He felt like spending all the cash on a ring was worth avoiding the emotional confrontation of not wanting to marry her. It wasn't a very well thought out plan, but I empathize with his short-term desperation. It's like plugging a leaky boat with a diamond, when what you really need is a different boat.

I'm technically responsible for the dissolution of their relationship. We were in the room one day and Jonah, another writer, brought his wife, Lorelei, in to visit him at work. Lunch in a writers' room was a time to indulge in our latest food fetish and ridicule someone; in this case Cubby and his life choices. This day was like most others, except that Jonah's wife was, for whatever series of clearance glitches, actually in the sanctum sanctorum with us.

While you might practice discretion at your office, in the room, we had a wilding of the truth. So, when someone started talking about a coed baby shower, I blurted out to Cubby that he shouldn't take Beth with him. It was too cruel to celebrate something so lovely and intimate with Beth, when he was dragging his emotional feet about the wedding. I forgot that Lorelei was friendly with Beth. She registered this, and slipped Beth the information. Lorelei told Beth that everyone in the writers' room seemed to understand a basic fact about her life that she didn't know herself yet: Cubby was very ambivalent about her, despite his two-and-a-half carat "commitment."

Cardinal rule: what is said in the room, stays in the room. Regardless, a domino was pushed over that day, and they all fell in rapid succession. Beth ended it with Cubby. Cubby was sad but relieved. He blamed me and then, two awkward weeks later, thanked me. Classy as always, Beth handed back the ring. Beth very quickly found the love of her life, and they are married now. Cubby has also gotten married to an even deeper version of the emotionally inaccessible, WASPY pretty type. Hope his new wife's not the second-guessing "I could've done better" type that he was.

All this is to say, these two people who genuinely cared for each other weren't right together. Both were trudging forward in lockstep. They needed a fender-bender with the truth. That was me, I guess. Had Cubby only been more honest within his relationship, it wouldn't have had to go that far. But, the thing that was supposed to happen, happened. Two unhappy people became four happy people.

Those annoying phrases—"everything happens for a reason," "there are no accidents," "silver linings," "meant to be"—that entire jar of thinking is true. Life is a series of opportunities for growth, but you can miss some of these moments if you resist change. You keep your head down, content with the thing that's broken because at least it's familiar. So, please, don't be begrudgingly/reluctantly locked into a bad thing, trying to be a "nice" guy. *Because you're locking someone else away from their good thing, too.*

Share your feelings. Give her the respect of knowing what you really think about her. Maybe the way in which she responds to your openness/fears is just the thing you were looking for in order to feel more connected to her. Or maybe she was just about to dump your ambivalent ass. Either way, we are back to truth and openness.

All this being said, if you still want to play emotional possum, it's easy. To end your relationship like a scared little boy, just stop giving, keep taking. To quicken this hideous process, go ahead and double up on helpings, you selfish noncommunicator. If your relationship is like that car analogy I mentioned earlier, stop taking it in for checkups. Drive it when the check engine light is on. No gas, no oil, no maintenance. Keep driving it until the thing breaks. Because it will. People do this to avoid an actual confrontation, but this is the most hurtful and time-consuming breakup method of all. And really, it's for pussies. Love her and yourself enough to be honest about your feelings. It's okay to have regrets; just say them aloud to the person they affect the most. It's okay to make mistakes. It's why Amazon has such a generous return policy.

On a personal note about breakups. I fought with every inch I had in order to hold on to something that wasn't right and wasn't sustaining. And in finally letting go, it opened up something I didn't know I needed to have: a complete life. Remember the kettle fight? Who knew that I could have it all. Breakups make room for what you didn't know you were missing. You learn to make do with a life that is not right for you. You imbue someone with false qualities, ones you wish they possessed, and then are angry at them for being who they are. She was always, still is, exactly who she was; I just never accepted that in her. I'm sorry, fictionally named Sarah.

The Three-Point Plan for Breaking Up

Okay, so here's what you're waiting for: the direct method of breakup. I warn you, it's not easy. However, I can guarantee that it will only be extremely uncomfortable for a short period of time, versus perpetually uncomfortable for an entire lifetime.

It is a three-point plan. You may not need all three, but you should have them all sharpened and ready in your quiver, just in case. It doesn't matter how long you've been with this person; without exception, break up face to face. No texting a breakup, unless you want to be that "asshole texting guy" forever in her history. And, in person, you may get to get in one last, emotionally resonant fuck. The tear-soaked-sheet finale.

I don't always recommend this one-last-fuck method, because it can be tricky. She may have a different agenda (the reel-you-back agenda) than you, but it is very difficult to walk away from. It naturally has sexy gravitas all over it because it's the last of something. So every kiss and thrust can be memorized and made into something poetic. It will be emotional for both of you, so don't confuse that feeling of fleeting connection with falling in love again. *You've ached over this conversation much longer than it takes you to come as the result of it.* It feels extra amazing because it is over, not because it is beginning. My recommendation is to do it only if you make sure it really is the last time. Don't bargain with your penis; he is a CIA agent. He will say and do anything to gain access. Once he's inside, he takes what he wants, gets out, and then detonates the area. If you don't want to blow up the person you once loved, be careful with this emission impossible.

The Tactical Breakup

POINT ONE: *"I care about you too much to keep doing this dance."*

This puts her needs first, or at least it sounds that way. It reminds her that you do care about her, even though you've gone as far as you can with her emotionally. Don't forget that as soon as this conversation is over, you won't need to do the untangling of her emotions with her. You will drive somewhere and drink beer with a friend who won't make you process your emotions. But right now, your job is to be emotionally clear and present and responsible. Soon it will be over. Soon there will be hot wings.

But, for now, all you have to do is lay out your interior thoughts in a kind and respectful manner. You are speaking your emotions out loud, not making her guess or project how you feel by how distant you've been. Say it with words, even though you know they will hurt her. Then the handoff of information becomes hers to deal with. You can't change your feelings; you've done all you can by communicating them. Her friends will now think you've finally manned up and been responsible to your feelings. Real truth is the universal get-out-of-jail-free card.

POINT TWO: *"This relationship isn't right for me, and that's never going to change."*

These are two important thoughts joined together in one sentence. Repeat them as necessary. Over and over if she needs that. You can also say the same thing using different words, as this is a big concept for her to grasp if she's still into you. So say this seventeen times, in whatever ways you can come up with. Say it decisively with no wiggle room. Adding phrases like "I don't think I can do this anymore . . ." provides loopholes. She only hears that there's a chance to make this work. "I can't do this anymore" is a very different revelation. Add the last part declaratively and decisively: "And that's never going to change." That means that you've really weighed this and thought it through. It's fairly inarguable, even if she prefers it weren't true.

Maybe you want to soften the blow. Maybe you're a big baby and say something like "I need a break." Or "This relationship needs a break." Very rarely does a break from a relationship turn into anything but a break*up*. More often, these demi-steps just provide a purgatory, with neither of you healing or moving forward, because you're still hoping that you can fix things. Or it can also be a true dissonance of communication where he hears "taking a break" as a breakup, and she hears it as simply "taking a break." This can lead to further screaming and arguments and hurt feelings, so trust me when I say, do it clean. Clarity is best. Stick to the script. Know that it's selfish to hold her emotionally hostage by giving yourself a little wiggle room in case you might want her back at some point in the future. Have the courage of your convictions. If it's over, it's over.

Only use Point Three if she just can't fucking grasp what it is you're saying directly in Point Two. Point Three is hurtful and difficult, but also sometimes very necessary. It is the nuclear bomb of breakup war. *Only use number three if there are no other options left, and the previous two points have failed.*

POINT THREE: *"I'm not in love with you, and I never will be."*

Fucking ouch. But very clarifying for the woman on the receiving end. When someone is done with someone, they are generally truly done. It takes two desiring people to have a relationship; anything less is not going to work. Your driver's ed teacher said it a million times: "Ambivalence kills." He was right. Ambivalence kills every emotion, but most especially love. So be selfish and state your true scary feelings, because you once loved this woman. She deserves the clarity of your conviction. In the end, your selfishness is actually selfless.

What to Do If She Breaks Up with You

Oh, wait. What if the unthinkable, unspeakable happens, and your woman actually breaks up with you? She's over you. She's had enough of your monosyllabic, monoemotional grunts that take her for granted. She's had enough of your sly booger picking and unabashed testicle adjusting. There's got to be someone better than you out there for her. But how can this be? You're great. Adorable, even. You're just so misunderstood. You have so many big feelings about her. Feelings that you may not have actually said aloud or shown her in any discernible way, but she should've intuited that you possess them.

Okay, so now she's dumped you. How do you get her back? That depends on a few things. No relationship between two people is ever really over unless someone is in some way abusive or there's a third party. So, if both of you are free of these, the potential exists for you to get back together. Maybe her breaking up with you was just the nudge you needed in order to clarify your feelings about her. So, there are a couple of things you can do here. Either be eternally wounded that she has broken up with you and never speak to her again. Or, go to her and share all of your feelings with her.

I have known so many guys who wind up marrying the woman who came directly after their first real heartbreak. They always regret not having opened up to the woman who harmed them. Their current relationship lives in the shadow of what might have been with the previous woman. I think this heartbreak is what shows men the capacity for how much they can actually feel. Only in the woman's absence do they feel her value. Their wound winds up being instructive. It teaches them what loss feels like, so they can go out into the world and find fulfillment. In this way, heartbreak is helpful. Don't forget that the heart is actually a muscle, and it gets stronger with more exercise.

So, if you're really into this woman and she's gotten rid of you—go to her and share your feelings. What's the downside? You look like an asshole? So what? Regrets only come from not having done something. Tell her what you haven't ever shared. Tell her what makes you scared. Tell her exactly what you're willing to change if she gives you another chance. And then actually, actively do it. Don't be full of shit here. If you get complacent, or lazy or internal or lurch along in life, the same thing will happen again. And maybe not even with this woman.

Perhaps you took this lesson of thwarted love and went onto the next with a "fuck her" attitude. And you didn't learn a damn thing from it. Your personality does again what it has always done. Your new woman will tire of it, too. Maybe she'll endure it for a longer period of time, but unless you evolve, you will face the same situation again and again until you shift something inside yourself. You can look all over the globe for the perfect woman, but big, huge bulletin here: you have to drag yourself along on this quest. You are you. You are going to make the same mistakes, pick the same kind of person, unless something in you clicks forward. You may find a new person who is less troubled by your lack of communication, and maybe that relationship will last a lifetime. But unless you can grow at least a little, you'll be broken, if not broken up with.

Chapter 10

For Women Only
Insights from an Insider

"Everything's great now. He understands he can man-handle
his private parts, but he has to woman-handle mine."

Wow, you people have been very patiently waiting your turn. And I know you usually put your needs second in lots of situations, so you may be used to it. Maybe your boyfriend/husband/baby-daddy bought this book; well, good for him. Even better for you. Or, maybe you bought it for him with the promise to read it to him aloud while naked. Not that he has been listening if you are naked. You have learned in these chapters that he's barely listening at all. Or, maybe you bought this book for you—not because you want to know how to fuck a woman, but because you want to know that someone out there can understand you, even if it's not the person you're in a relationship with. Someone knows how to crack your code. Whatever the reason, I know the whole book is about women, but I wanted to address a chapter to you directly.

See, the penis is like a blind man's skin cane, moving forward in pursuit of the same cozy, warm opening it experienced when first entering the world. But actually we're all in pursuit of the same thing. Women seek primal arms to hold them. Men search for primal walls to contain them. You just need more information in order to get what you both want.

The hardest thing about being attracted to my own gender is that I have to play by the same rules that I hand out. And, as much as I know that my opinions are accurate, that doesn't mean I can always implement them myself, because I am also a woman. Sometimes I disregard my own advice because my own girl emotions force me to supersede it.

How to Find Balance in Your Relationship

I distribute reels of advice to my friends:

> Don't ask too many questions. I know, you want to be asked about stuff! Men don't! They want to be left to their own thoughts!
> Don't take it all so personally, he's probably not even thinking about you.
> His silence is reparative; don't project just because your silence is punitive. He's not thinking about you—or if he is, he doesn't want to talk about it because his bad feelings will evaporate if you don't try to dig into his brain. So just avoid it and lie low.
> Compliment him, or better yet, blow him.

Don't pout when he doesn't want to French kiss
you. That's for birthdays and anniversaries, or
when you're both a little drunk and can pretend to be kissing somebody else.
If he's at home, don't bug him about work,
don't nag him about stuff he hasn't accomplished, don't compare him; just accept him
as less complicated.
And stop processing and taking personally what
he *doesn't* say.

Ahh, all so true. My friends nod when hearing this
type of spot-on advice. "Ah, God, you're so right about me.
That is what I do. Sometimes, I make it so much worse. I'll
apply this ointment to my own inflamed personality
immediately." But they don't, because they can't. And that
creates a balance in male-female relationships. He resents
you for feeling so much, but he loves you because you feel
so much, which, in turn, forces *him* to feel. Even if that
feeling is "annoyed."

All of my extremely good advice is totally lost on me,
though. When I am in a daze of hurt feelings or hormonal
blasts, I can't think straight. I can't be reasoned with, even
if I'm the one who ordinarily provides the reasoning. I
make the same mistakes that I just warned my friends
against making. And even worse, in a relationship of two
women, we don't trade sex for the emotional "out" of a
confrontation. I hear this from my straight friends all the

time; sex becomes a form of currency. "I'm scared for my husband to see the credit card bill! I spent way too much money on a purse. I'm going to have to blow him to get out of trouble."

Wait, what? Is this normal for you people? Or, "I accidentally left the house this morning with my boyfriend's car keys in my purse, so I'm going to have to fuck him tonight." Huh? Two women in a relationship together simply don't engage in this type of sexual barter. Though I most certainly respect it and decidedly long for it, it just doesn't exist as an option. I wish to God it did. It would be so much simpler to just fuck away the bad feelings, versus having to endure a bleary-eyed marathon.

Her: "When you left the house with my car keys in your messenger bag, it felt like you didn't *see* me. Like I'm invisible. And then I had to spend my day correcting your mistake by Ubering to your office to get my own keys. That's because you think you've got more going on work-wise than I do, which makes me feel less-than . . ." Oh my God, if *only* there was a secret oral sex exit out of this level of hellish emotional brick breaking. But it isn't the way women are constituted.

The Truth from an Inside Trader/Traitor

Okay, a little background about me. Who knows if I was born gay? If I was, it was obscured by the pinkity-pink of the dresses I was shoved into without a care as to my opinion. As I grew up, I kind of followed what my peers were doing, and that included exploring my sexuality with the opposite sex. Heterosexual seduction was like a very easy game; one, it seemed, boys would let you win.

As my sexuality evolved into wanting women, sexual conquest was less triumphant. Even as a female, the quest for girls was always more complicated, the thirst never as easily satisfied. Simply, women are more emotionally complicated than men. Even if you know the inner workings of a girl because *you are* a girl, there are no gimmes. Not unless you are the fictional *Friday Night Lights* character, Tim Riggins. If you are Tim Riggins, you may stop reading and continue fucking.

For this reason, my straight lady friends love to pepper me with "Is it true that . . ." types of questions. Like I'm the answer key, the Teacher's Edition, to what men think and feel. Like I'm willing to be an inside trader. And the truth is, I am. Sure, I like girls, but I am one first, so my allegiance is with us. I do know stuff about guys that women may want to know, because I walk fairly invisibly behind the "enemy" lines. And I am happy to share this stuff with you. Guys tell me things I really don't want to know. Didn't ask to know. Can't shake off, once I do know.

But women also ask me things they wouldn't, and couldn't, ask a man. They conjecture to me as if I'm a guy with a higher capacity for comprehension. They muse, "If you're attracted to women, do you spend a lot of time touching your own breasts?" "If you're into girls, why aren't you into me? *Are* you into me?" "Guys make a lot of jokes about how women smell and taste; are those rumors true?

Are we gross?" All those terrible jokes men cling to because guys want to receive and not give oral sex. Those innuendos have had women throughout the ages wondering about the aromatic nature of our own genitals.

Answers: I lost interest in my own boobs a long time ago. You always want what you don't have. No, I am not attracted to most heterosexual women, because being with a woman who has never been with a woman is a little like teaching someone how to ice skate. Skating only gets fun after you're done with the lengthy initial insecurities and instruction process. You want to skate with someone who has let go and found her own balance and style. And, as for the mythology of the scent of a woman: well, if for some reason it's strong, there's generally something going on down there. In their pristine state, vaginas are delightful.

What We Say versus What Men Hear

Here's what we sound like to men: the dull, teasing, incessant whine of a housefly. This fly will neither die nor be hit with what was once a magazine, and is now probably one of a pair of flip-flops. I know this because I often am like this. I like to have sex with women, but genetics win here; I *am* one. I am a buzzy housefly.

Here's some good advice: the only way to stop this annoying habit is to quit whining and nagging and dwelling on expressing whatever it is you don't currently possess. Inside your head or aloud, stop fucking complaining all the time. Stop saying it's hot when it's hot, or cold when it's cold. No one exclaims when it's the perfect temperature. No one needs to hear this constant emotional status report of what's going on for you at any given moment.

Be gentle with your words, and with your actions. Be grateful for what you have, and express that out loud, using specifics. Do something caretaking. This can be food preparation or extra thoughtfulness in your work, or exercise or sexual desire or generosity. If you have to complain, call your friends—they'll interrupt you with their own problems, which may even sound worse than yours.

Clear Your History

Let your boyfriend or husband watch whatever the hell he wants to watch on TV. It doesn't matter if you don't enjoy a documentary about Nikola Tesla; just step up your game and stop kvetching—just watch your own thing on your laptop. I literally can't get enough of the Housewives of all the Bravo states, but men can. The Housewives are the composite of his greatest fears: yelling, plastic surgery, wigs, backstabbing, shit-talking, spending, fighting, wine-soaked lunches, matched sets of costly luggage, beach houses, wire fraud, gossiping, and lack of satisfaction despite enormous wealth—and all of it in a world where nannies are watching the children 24/7.

Stop bringing up old issues, remembering old details and using them against him. Clear your history of these events. Either forgive and move on, or literally move on.

There is no yesterday. We only have today and tomorrow, so make today fresh and new.

Contain your web of complex thoughts. Rope them in, shush them like a crying infant. This vessel of fears and list of things you have to accomplish is the buzzing of the fly. If you can't totally shut up, just know that the fly is way less annoying if it is just flitting noiselessly. So stop being so negative. Do it. Do it even if it hurts to do it. Bite the insides of your cheeks and pretend to be an entirely different person than you are if you have to. Act as-if, pretend to be better than you are, and see whether gradually things start to shift. Mostly, don't misinterpret what he *isn't* saying as what he is feeling. Don't take things he doesn't say personally—after all, he never said them.

In his silence, he may even be feeling something positive about you. Then, you add your own lens, distort it, layer in your own fictional narrative and historical baggage and emotional cologne, which makes him defensive. It will drive him away.

Don't Assume He Understands

The most important thing I've noticed about all relationships is the idea that we assume our partner *should* understand us. We imbue him/her with the ability to mind read, and then are offended when he/she is not a crystal ball–gazing soothsayer. I hear this all the time from my friends in varying degrees: "He should know how I feel! After all this time, how can he not know?!"

Okay, but he doesn't, and he can't. What is obvious to you is not obvious to him. You come with your own wiring and, like it or not, speak with a language that is truly foreign to him. "Why are you asking me if there's more toothpaste, when I'm talking about how I feel about not being included on a task team I wanted to be on at work?" "Are you not listening to me?" "Do you not have feet that can walk to the medicine cabinet and check yourself?" "You know the answer to that question; you buy toothpaste at a place called the grocery store. Same location they sell vodka, so I'd think you'd be more familiar with it."

Truth: when women's voices reach a certain sharp pitch, men's brains switch to hearing "blappity blap blappity blap"—even if she is shouting the winning Lotto numbers. No matter what she's saying, because of how she is saying it, they simply are not listening. I've watched football for more than a dozen years, but still don't know what all those stupid hand signals the referees make mean. I've given up wanting to figure them out. Instead, I've learned to listen to the sounds of the crowd. If the crowd cheers after the ref's hand gestures and that's the team I'm rooting for, I know to be happy. Same thing for you. Even *after* telling him how you feel, he may not get it.

Masturbation Doesn't Mean He Loves You Less

Here's another important thing to understand: before guys were men, they were boys. Boys love to masturbate. Any second that they are alone in the world, they're playing with their dicks. And men do this, too. Not much about this changes. Of the men I surveyed, most said self-stimulation relaxed them and relieved stress, and they didn't want to bug their girlfriends or wives for a couple minutes of purely selfish pleasure. A man loves to play Madden, but cock fondling is his original sport. I mean, Eve gets a lot of credit and blame for offering up the allegorical apple in Eden but, even without her, Adam would've come across this forbidden piece of fruit and fucked it until it was cored.

Listen up, ladies: men do not love their woman less because they jerk off. It has zero to do with how often you fuck him or how rich you perceive your sex life to be. This is simply their way of quick release. It is a relationship they've had for a very long time, and they wouldn't want to disappoint their penis. It reminds them that they are still free, still alive. It quiets their constantly whirring motor. They do this so they can get back to listening to you, playing an idiotic game with their kids, remaining upright during a boring dinner with your judgmental friends who discuss nothing that ever interests them. They must release, and so they do.

But take a journey with me to their boyhoods, when their pubescent sacs really start thumping. It must be so distracting to all of a sudden receive higher and higher surges of testosterone, and not know what to do with it. Their bodies are developing faster than their social skills, and it's way too early for physical contact with the other gender, so they find release through self-stimulation.

Okay, fine, but walk down this path with me for a second. Let's do the simple math, here. These boys achieve erection just because they're wearing a slightly less worn-in pair of boxer briefs, and are used to satisfying themselves in several delightful strokes. These same young men are supposed to suddenly understand how to pleasure a female person. But their wiring is whacked. It is conditioned for speed, not stamina. It is a practice designed for release, to not get caught by a snoopy parent or sneaky sibling while covertly jacking it. So this same muscle, the one they've spent endless hours privately honing during puberty . . . is the same one they take to game day. And speed is generally the opposite of what a woman desires sexually.

So okay, the much anticipated day arrives when they finally have some type of sexual interaction with a woman. What do you think is going to happen? Well, they have no clue what to do with this real live person. They are only used to unrealistic visual stimuli via the computer, fantastical mental pictures, or substandard descriptions from peers.

They have no clue sexually, physically, or otherwise what to do with this enigmatic thing that is a vagina. And to be honest, at that point in their fucking careers, they don't really care. They want release. Just like they did all over the bathroom/bed/car/garage/shower/toilet/sock/soft sandwich-bread/wig while practicing for the big day. It's just that they were practicing for the wrong thing. They know how to jerk themselves off very well in no time flat. Anywhere, and utilizing anything. Even at fourteen, boys are creative, resourceful, and industrious in terms of innovating ersatz vaginas. They are the MacGyvers of masturbation. But ask them to come up with a unique anniversary gift for the mother of their kids, and they want a knees-on-the-ground ovation for roses and baby's breath wrapped in cellophane purchased at the gas station convenience market.

Since boyhood, these guys have been overly familiar with themselves. Through practice, they know their way around this thing that alternately dangles and thunders between their legs. They know exactly what *they* want. But wait. Now they're supposed to please a female. Well, the first time they meet a vagina, pleasuring it has got to be their eightieth concern. They are thinking, "Yessssss, I can't believe I'm here!" "I made it to the Bigs!" "Right this second I am having a rite of passage!" "I'm now in the club of knowing!" "Omigod, this feels so wet and weird and messy and crazy and different from mine and omigod!" "I can't wait to tell my friends!"

But all of that is super secondary, superseded by the larger, physiological drumbeat of their nuts and dick: "Goodfeelgoodfeelcumcumcum!" Their major concern— beyond what boobs *actually* feel like or this new weird orifice in front of them—is not blowing an accidental load on her leg, or even before they can get their dick out of their underpants.

Go Easy on the Critique of His Technique

So, this is some approximation of his first time. After that, his partner is trying not to crush his tender young ego, but instead is just encouraging him to do what he's doing. After all, the social dynamics of a burgeoning sexuality are shameful and weird and competitive . . . so why would a young teenage girl going through her own list of primal firsts go, "No, no, you're doing that all wrong!" or "Ow! No, that hurts, you're too ON IT, ouch!" or "Don't squeeze my boobs so hard, they're attached to me! They aren't two blobs of pizza dough!" "No, I guess you man-handle your dick like that, but my private area requires woman-handling."

Girls, like guys, are just blooming, too, so now is the opportunity for girls to develop their own emotional deftness. They want to be loved, to fit in, to be adored. So why would they take this, their actual first opportunity, to literally bust balls? So our primary physical interaction is the blind leading the kind. That is how men develop what it is they do in bed (or car). And by the time women have the ego strength to offer up even gentle thoughtful hints or suggestions, men's habits are solidified.

For the brave and heroic women and girls who helped instruct their boyfriends on what they actively like: good for you. Because sometimes guys will dump anyone they perceive as critical. Women are simply trying to tell him what they like, but of course he's going to take it personally; it's super personal. It's what he's *not* doing that is displeasing her. The woman is attacking the guy at his core, his nuts, where he actually *lives*. It's all embarrassing and new and vulnerable. So go easy on your guy when you're critiquing his moves. And have him read chapter 8 of this book.

How to Know Which Guys to Avoid

There are many types of guys to avoid when deciding to start dating someone. But sometimes, you have to scratch the surface to find out who they really are. If I could draw labels on their foreheads in Sharpie pen, I would say to avoid the following. Again, this list is by no means comprehensive; feel free to add to it.

- The guy who you wish was more into you.
- The fuck buddy who you wish would become more.
- The guy who won't grow up. Peter Panstein.
- The half-truth guy.
- The man who won't say I love you.
- The short-term serial monogamist.
- The scared-to-commit guy.
- The commits-too-fast guy.
- The super-pursuer.
- The guy who won't text back.
- The guy who is prettier than you.
- The guy who isn't even in your league.
- The super-sarcastic.
- The too-earnest.
- The crier (I know this can sound good at first; he's emotional, that's nice. But if he's crying all the time, chances are his tears aren't even about you. They are about the fact that no one was around to wipe them away originally. Or

maybe someone was always around to wipe them away, so he never got a chance to do it for himself. Either way, this is too much for you to handle in a partner.)

- Too many exes.
- Too few exes.
- Too many kids.
- Doesn't want to entertain the idea of having kids.
- The one with too much to prove.
- The one who doesn't have enough to prove.
- The workaholic.
- The slacker.
- The too-small-penised—and yes . . . I know it's hard to fathom, but also . . .
- The too-big-penised.
- The guy who thinks he has all the answers.
- The guy who doesn't bother asking the questions.
- The mama's boy.
- The daddy's boy.
- The separated guy. (I feel like I don't even have to mention the married guy, but avoid this one, too. He lives in an odd place that indicates he knows how to commit to marriage, but he also can't commit to divorce.)
- The too-confident.
- The too-insecure.
- The guy who reminds you of your ex, your dad, or your brother.

- The broke guy.
- The out-every-night guy.
- The guy who doesn't want to leave the house.
- The secretive man.
- The oversharing man.
- The one who doesn't like your job, your hair, your friends, your family, your cat, your height, and your knuckles.
- The one who tells you that you can't do something; who doesn't encourage you to follow your dreams.
- The one who will let you live in your delusional ambitions when they are way past the point of failing dangerously.

I get it. After this list, it leaves pretty much no one. But they are out there. Don't be content to just scour the dregs of a club or be the friend who got dragged along with your best friend's new boyfriend's friend. This is an important choice that affects you for forever, so pick well and go slowly. Don't waste your time on those who steal your energy, or who you know aren't the right one. Sure, it's fun to go have a good time. It's fun to fuck whomever you want, too. But just be careful. If you're with the wrong person for too long, it can sidetrack your life from being the one you've always wanted for yourself. Wasting time with the wrong person can steal time away from the path you're actually supposed to be on. Every penis is a choice.

An example of someone not to date: About seven years ago, my friend Melissa, an extremely bright woman with equally bright green eyes, was excited to introduce me to her new boyfriend. We went out to lunch. He was nice enough. Paid for his food with a debit card. His wallet was held together with yellow duct tape. He wore too-light denim, too-plaid shirt. No watch. Didn't even check the time on his phone. He ordered blueberry pie with ice cream. As his entree.

Afterwards, Melissa pestered me for approval: "What'd you think? Isn't Matt great? Isn't he so, so great?" She wanted to hear that I liked him, but I had all the clues I needed. So I did what any true friend would do: I told her the truth. Matt was an adult baby with a still-soft fontanel. He was in his thirties and wore shoes with no laces, as if on suicide watch. His keychain had a "BevMo" mini–credit card thingie on it next to his "Go Packers" beer bottle opener.

Melissa was stunned. I pushed on, with no mercy. "He used the word 'awesome' regarding the discovery of the hatch on *Lost*." I pronounced him not ripe for adult expectations. My friend was mad at *me*, but all I did was tell her the truth. After *she* asked me.

Naturally, Melissa married him. She should've listened to me. She couldn't read the signposts. They weren't written in Lesbianese, but so what if they were; I *translated* all of this stuff for her. I warned her that Matt was a man-boy. He'd sit down on the tile floor while showering, as if life was just too tiring to be upright while warm water splashed on his sudsy shoulders. He left shit-skids on the back of his tighty-whities. He wouldn't hug Melissa because he said it was a waste of time "if nothing was going to happen." He was an adult baby. And so, when I heard about Melissa and Matt's divorce years later, to me it had already happened. I wish she would've listened, and I'll bet she does, too. She pays him child support. And the kids didn't even get her green eyes.

A Few More Types to Avoid

Women, while you're busy searching the world for the one, avoid the depressed, the loners, and the guy who has obvious fixable physical flaws that he just doesn't bother to deal with because "it's just the way I am."

I know of only one exception to this theory. My friend Claire's boyfriend had this dead front tooth. You know, one of the big ones. He had the money to fix it. And yet it hung there for years, like some ignored boarded-up window in a building no one wanted to lease. I always wondered about Dead Tooth's crazy level of internal self-worth and confidence, as in "Claire will love me with or without a cosmetic repair." Or maybe it wasn't hubris; maybe it was even crazier: maybe he didn't even notice it himself. Is that even possible? I mean, didn't he see it while he was shaving or flossing in the crevices around all its glorious deadness?

Claire noticed it, but she thought he might be self-conscious about it, so she never mentioned it to him. For years. Very restrained of her. I admired this, but would never have had the self-control not to say anything. It was all I could do to stop myself from blurting it out every time we went to dinner: "Oh hey, would you mind passing the dead tooth." "Sure, I'd love another dead tooth . . ." "I checked out the dessert menu . . . anyone up for splitting a little dead tooth?"

So, much like all dead things, the dead tooth continued to be dead until one day, Dead Tooth proposed to sweet Claire. When Claire's French mother learned the news about their engagement, she quickly decried, very first thing, to his face, oh so matter-of-fact: "*Très bien*. You're to be married. Now. What are we going to do about that dead tooth?" And it was just like that. He fixed it before the wedding. Claire and Veneer are still happily married all these many years later. But that's the only exception to the rule. Don't go bending the rule if you don't have to.

If you have the entire world to choose from, why would you pick an old man if you are a young woman? Don't do it if you don't have to. You've seen it before: a dusty, fragile stick figure of a man, skull and crossbones–style osteoporotic hand, arthritically bulbous knuckled, who's with a buxom phony-titted beauty. She is scoping out his house for shit to steal when he dies, before his kids can do an inventory of the place. You've seen them out for dinner. You assume they are father and daughter or even grandfather and granddaughter. You take solace in the fact that she's kind enough to spend time with her elder relation. What a nice family. And then they French kiss.

I once asked an overly plastic-surgeried and perfumed woman what her type was, and she said, "Rich and sickly."

There are also men who aim so far above their heads that they ignore women who would be perfect for them. I had this not-so-handsome friend who used to say, "The heart wants what it wants." He had a type; he'd pine away for the prettiest girl in the room; the one with the thickest lips, most stacked ass, and highest heels. He'd say, shrugging, "I'm attracted to who I'm attracted to." He didn't get it, but this was a recipe for total frustration. He's still alone. Just because you want what you want doesn't mean it's good for you, or that you'll wind up getting it. Which sets up a string of heartbreaking frustration. Which sets you up to think that's what love is supposed to feel like. Love is actually supposed to feel satisfying. It's not the more complicated tributary of love, which is called yearning.

No One Ever Changes More Than 15 Percent

Often, women are attracted to a certain type of man, one that they believe they can change. They think they possess a powerful enough tonic to shift this guy's lifelong personality. Please watch out for this type. You won't ever change him, but ultimately, the quest to change him will change you.

An example of the type of guy a woman wants to change is someone I'll call Truman—whose real name is *almost* as cool as that (but both names are far cooler than he is). Truman always tells me with great astonishment that he has been suckered into dating yet another "not a great girl."

All of his stories are the same; they're just flavored differently. Me: "What did you do last night?" Him: "I ended up going to a party." Then he nudges me with his elbow. "I may still be buzzed." I do the math: 1. Yesterday was Tuesday. 2. Buzzed means high. 3. We are at work. Keep in mind this guy is easily in his early forties. He's marginally handsome, certainly for a writer. He is a modern-day Topher Columbus, a vaginal explorer, credited with discovering new lands. And he implies that he's doing it for the good of the rest of the men in the room.

Truman's stories are about a secret after-hours club, a secret after-club-after-party he was invited to (*what* is it after? Life?). The invention of new and incredible drugs that the rest of us haven't yet had a chance to sample, because we are eating a pointy toast sandwich at the American Girl Doll Bistro with our daughters and their identically dressed doll counterparts.

The stories usually include a couple of vague celebrities. Not the right ones. Sometimes, something about the Playboy Mansion. All delivered tantalizingly to the married boys. As if the Playboy Mansion isn't owned by an octogenarian with octogenarian friends and old guy–type furniture and odors. I've been there. Not to be a huge buzzkill, but it's like a retirement home sprinkled with freshly waxed, siliconed and V05'd twenty-year-olds. But, in real life, most of the regular guests at the Mansion are very old men and women. Basically, it's a retirement home for people who once had tons of crazy sex. In the 1970s, maybe pipe-smoking, raven-haired Hef in his satin rabbit-insignia'd robe was sexy. But now he's an old dude—droopy balls banging around in his pj's while still being escorted around by a wife sixty years his junior. These aren't your parents here; they're your grandparents. Would you ever go hang out with your grandparents' friends reminiscing about the good old days when they were 69'ing each other on cocaine?

But Truman and the other guys in the writers' room aren't listening to my tales of spying reel-to-reel audio systems or banged-up faux-wood-paneled game rooms. They don't want to hear my version; they only want to listen lustfully to Truman's stories, which illustrate why he will never change. They listen, aching, like they've fucked up their whole lives by marrying one person and making responsibility-inducing children with her.

I'm the one who asks the provocative questions here. Truman says he was late to work because he had a fight with the girl that he hooks up with sometimes. We've heard about her before. We call her "the hot bi-girl." Believe me, there are plenty of not-so-hot bi-girls, but we cling to this one. We've seen iPhone pictures that Truman promised her he'd never show.

Truman thinks that if he fucks bi-girl a couple times a month, he can still continue his quest to find the mythical "great girl." But he's been searching a while and according to his calculations, there don't seem to be any. "How old is

Hot-Bi?" I ask, mental fingers crossed. He is vague. "Early twenties." I see. I wonder what someone can possibly argue about with a twenty-two-year-old? Sour Patch vs. Gummy Bears?

He tells me they had a fight because his condom broke, and he panicked. "Well, why'd you fight? She didn't want to take the morning-after pill?" I joke. This startles him. "Wait, what? Do you think she should?" "*Should?*" I marvel. I thought that was why he was late for work. I figured he had to drive to the drugstore and then back again to watch her take it and check under her tongue to make sure she swallowed it like a lothario Nurse Ratched.

Truman now turns even greener than the boozy hue he came in with today. Says he'll text Hot-Bi, have her pick it up, he'll reimburse her, he's sure it'll be cool. I wonder if maybe he *wants* to have a baby with this crazy baby. After all, I know she's very young and beautiful. So young that the only thing she's left unpierced is her bisexuality; so young that her father (who is two years younger than Truman) is serving a jail sentence. I assume he must be making this up. I laugh. "As long as it's not for murder." Truman corrects me unironically, "Manslaughter."

Now I'm worried that Truman has impregnated a murderer's daughter. I'm no longer laughing at his sex-ploits with an oh-well, good-natured rubber-necking atti-tude. I am worried for his safety and also his paycheck. I urge him to go to the drugstore. Get a pill (cheaper to pay for a pill than college tuition!). The men want to know about her boobs, which are big, by the way. No one wonders if she has a big vagina. Which, in case you don't know, is way less good.

Now, keep in mind—I enjoy having sex with my own gender. But this is what separates the men from the girls. I don't look at pretty first and then the red flags. To me, they are all one package. I won't look at tits affixed to a host of insurmountable eternal headaches and go, "Oh, fuck it, there's always Valtrex." But men seemingly never learn this lesson.

The boys in the room are clamoring for details. "If she's bi, can you get a three-way?" Are we all missing the headline here? This large-busted child-woman is potentially carrying Truman's only progeny, and all these guys are concerned with is whether he got the chance to have anal. When I mention that there may be a child here, suddenly Truman experiences conflict. Maybe *this* is a sign. Maybe this will push his life in a direction that he alleges he wants, but never makes the necessary choices to pursue.

Now, Truman may have made a child with a hot-bi-twenty-two-year-old with a murderous dad, a woman only slightly older than an actual child; but he won't even text back the super-sweet fifth grade teacher he went out with last week. No. He "just wasn't into it; not his thing." Didn't like the looks of her hair. Too too itchy to sleep next to.

Truman is a smart man; brilliant by some standards. But he cannot see what is in front of him when camouflaged by a stark-ravingly-gorgeous vagina. So, while the boys murmur riotous envy in the room, I am quiet for a moment. Then I ask the hardest question: "When you are in the shower . . . finally by yourself after your long night and drunk morning of fucking . . . aren't you lonely?" His eyes get wet with tears. He probably won't even deny this; there were seven witnesses. He doesn't break my gaze, so grateful for this tiny second of feeling understood. He nods without nodding.

I move in, hug him. A slow, important hug. I mean this hug with all my heart. Not judgmental for a moment, for a change. Nothing condescending about it. He leans into me, allowing this, our embrace. I feel his weight relax into my own. I know he's moved by the simplicity of our connection. This hug is washing away all his stupid moves and poor decisions; this hug will change him forever. After this, he realizes the folly of his actions and will be ready for true love.

This hug cleanses everything. He lingers for a beat, then Truman says it aloud: "I need you to let go . . ." "Huh?" I stare at him, confused, as we stand an inch apart. After all this time, I've forgotten male physiology. I finally catch on, letting go. He shrugs, simply: he's half hard.

The gory truth is that men will never stop being men. Most of the change is in you. You have to be willing to try to stop changing them. Someone said, no one ever really changes more than 15 percent. So you'd better pick well enough to make sure that other 85 percent is pretty great.

It's Not Just About the Sex

Men and women: please put aside your genitals and everyone read the following. It's very important.

The thing is, your relationship can break unless you pay attention to the creaking along the way. Unless you change the way you approach her, or the way you approach him, something will force you to pay attention. Something will happen that you can no longer ignore or dismiss. But I hope that something sneaky has happened along the way here. If you've diligently read this book up to this point, maybe a few things will stick. How to listen. How to empty a trash can. How to finger-fuck. It doesn't matter. Any of these things will prove that you have the ability to change. And that tiny thing that is different about you will be the new thing in the petri dish. The one new idea that seeped into you will grow and maybe change everything. With only a few small movements, just like in fucking, you can crack the entire code. You can have it all. The part where you feel better about yourself exists in the places where you stretch and grow.

Sure, this stuff all seems like a bunch of love and sex tips—and it is. If you implement some of this stuff, sure, more people will come, which generally puts everyone in a better mood. But more importantly, more people will connect. And connection does bring change, healing, openness, and love. With love, like it or not, we grow.

So get out there. Put down your iPad. Turn off your Kindle. Stop reading this book while you're off pouting because of some idiotic miscommunication with the person you love and value. Go connect with your person. Different or not, if we're in this together, the world is ours.

Acknowledgments

I want to thank everyone at Weinstein books: Amanda Murray, Georgina Levitt and Kathleen Schmidt, who made this is as different and amazing a writing experience as I've ever had.

Thank you to my tireless and brilliant editor: Leslie Wells, the only person who gets less sleep than I do.

Thank you to so many people for so many years at WME: Ari Greenberg, Richard Weitz, Lisa Harrison. To the incomparable Andy McNicol, endlessly patient in the face of my fears.

Thank you to Soleil Moon Frye for laughing and then making me take this idea to Andy in the first place.

To my best friend Elaine Pope, my main dispensary of advice in all things wise and insightful, though she will avoid sexual matters at all costs. She is, after all, the Pope.

Thank you to my parents, Allan Adler and Frances Payne Adler. My brain is so much a product of their genetic mash-up: a psychiatrist and a poet. And to my stepmom Judy Adler, so much more than just a stepmom, but that's the title I'm limited to use.

Thank you to my brother, Michael Adler. And to Molly Newcomer, my sister-in-law and one of my closest friends. They are a role-model couple for me. Married for twenty-one years, they still kiss every day.

To Melody Young and Christy Snyder and Rhonda Endlund and Jared Levine and Alex Kohner and Cindy Comito for keeping it all together.

To all the women I've slept with and to those it never occurred to me to sleep with.

To all the hilarious, heart-shaping men along the way. Thank you for including me in your conversations.

Thank you to John Stamos, that I ever got to meet you and more or less consider you my friend. Blackie Parrish for President.

To Greg Berlanti, your wisdom is contained within your dimples. Both are very deep.

To Paul Downs Colaizzo, I will join whatever religion you one day choose to start.

To Ana Maza, whose insight and generosity makes so much in my life possible.

To my gaggle of forever female friends who shared their stories with me and still do. All the time. Women really love to talk. Melissa Berton, Aline Brosh McKenna, Jen Crittenden, Kate Adler, Sophia Rossi, Sarah Schechter, Carla Hacken, Howard Stern's penis, Dana Fox, Kelly Oxford, Jenni Konner, Carleen Cappelletti and the incomparable Kathy Greenberg.

To the teachers who told me I should write and then made me: Laura Michaels, Beverly White, Robert Litchfield and Michael Auer. Feels weird not to call them Mrs. And Mr.

To the Mount Rushmore of women who inspired me: Dorothy Parker, Fran Lebowitz, Gilda Radner and Sandra Bernhard.

To my love, Liz Brixius. Thank you for always giving me a soft place to land.

And, lastly, to my 97-year-old Oma who stopped speaking to me decades ago for being gay. Hope this has been a fun read.